Leading
for Wellness

Leading
for Wellness

HOW TO CREATE A TEAM CULTURE
WHERE EVERYONE **THRIVES**

Patricia Grabarek
Katina Sawyer

WILEY

Published by John Wiley & Sons, Inc., Hoboken, New Jersey.
Published simultaneously in Canada.

For general information on our other products and services or for technical support, please contact our Customer Care Department within the United States at (800) 762-2974, outside the United States at (317) 572-3993 or fax (317) 572-4002.

Wiley also publishes its books in a variety of electronic formats. Some content that appears in print may not be available in electronic formats. For more information about Wiley products, visit our web site at www.wiley.com.

Library of Congress Cataloging-in-Publication Data is Available:

ISBN 9781394292011 (Hardback)
ISBN 9781394292028 (epdf)
ISBN 9781394292035 (epub)

Cover Design: Jon Boylan
Author Photos by Vanie Poyey

SKY10097509_012925

To Daniel and Brendan:
For your unwavering support and understanding,
for making sure we stayed well while writing about wellness,
and for always believing in us

Contents

Introduction   *ix*

1 **Why Workplace Wellness Matters**   **1**

PART I NO ONE WANTS A SUPERHERO **17**

2 **Fire Your Work Self**   **19**

3 **Embrace Your Struggle Statement**   **37**

PART II IT'S THE TONE, NOT THE TIME **57**

4 **Set the Right Tone**   **59**

5 **Swiftly Become a Confidant**   **81**

PART III WORK SHOULD SUPPORT LIFE **105**

6 **Be Elastic: Your Way Isn't Always Right** **107**

7 **Become a Boundary Bouncer**   **131**

PART IV ONE SIZE DOESN'T FIT ALL **151**

8 **The Power of Person-Centered Planning** **153**

9 **Eliminating Mental Health Stigma**   **175**

PART V FINAL THOUGHTS AND ACTIONS   195

10 Challenges and Backlash   197

11 Action Planning   225

Notes   243
Acknowledgments   253
About the Authors   257
Index   259

Introduction

I look at wellness as: Do I have time to do my job well? Do I have things that I can do outside of work that are supported? Is there that feeling of family first, health first, and being a well-rounded individual? That, to me, is what wellness is from leadership. To have that comfort level of being able to have a well-rounded life. Sort of that saying: "Sound body, sound mind." I often feel like it's "Sound personal life, sound work life." And sometimes I do believe that it's [all] just life. It's not work, it's not personal, it's just my life. And I appreciate a boss and a leader that isn't saying I can do that but also lives it themselves.

—Mia, recruiting and training consultant, study participant

Consider for a moment Jayme, a talented veterinarian who is working long hours at her new clinic. The clinic is experiencing a big influx of new patients this year, keeping the staff extremely busy. Most people are working overtime and are exhausted. Employees recently completed an employee survey and were honest about feeling burned out. In response, the human resources team decided to launch training to improve employee wellness. They sent Jayme and her team members a link to a mandatory, online, four-hour resilience training. Jayme was told she had a week to complete the training, even though she had no time during work hours. Despite being depleted of energy by the end of the workweek, Jayme had to finish the training over the weekend to meet the deadline.

If you were Jayme, how would you feel? Would you feel heard by HR or frustrated? Do you think this solution would work? If you think this solution seems unreasonable and unhelpful, you aren't alone. Unfortunately, this is based on a true story—and the real-life "Jayme" (study participants' names have been changed throughout the book to protect confidentiality) felt extremely frustrated. The training felt like a quick check-the-box solution and didn't provide the real help clinic employees needed. In fact, in some ways, Jayme felt like the training made her wellness worse. She wasn't able to fully disconnect from work over the weekend; instead she had to devote four hours of her recovery time to even more work. This story is just one of many. You probably have your own examples of wellness programs implemented at work that felt more like insults than solutions.

Stories like Jayme's led us to write this book. We heard clients, friends, and colleagues complaining about stress at work, burnout, and the resulting impact on their companies, jobs, and well-being. No one seemed to know how to solve the problem. So we embarked on a hunt for the answers. We dug into the research, searching for concrete guidance to help. Although we found some great science that we will share throughout the book, there were still some unanswered questions. Even more concerning, there was no clear roadmap to follow to create a thriving work environment. Thus, we stepped in to bridge that gap.

At the heart of our research, we found that there's a mismatch between how employees and organizations define the term "wellness." Consider what wellness means to you. We asked this simple question to dozens of employees and got a range of responses—from a feeling of balance, to being seen as a whole person, to being able to turn the Zoom camera off and take a walk during a meeting. But one theme rang true throughout the data we gathered: Wellness is *not* an initiative or a program. Instead, we learned that wellness is improved when employees' day-to-day work conditions support their health and happiness, not a surface-level approach for addressing an otherwise stressful or overwhelming work environment. Yet so much of what companies invest in when they try to promote wellness focuses on individual-level, blanket solutions that address the by-products of stress and burnout instead of addressing the root causes of these workplace problems. This book is here to change how companies take action to improve workplace wellness.

Luckily, our data showed a clear path forward for creating the wellness-focused workplaces employees are looking for. *Leaders* are the most critical force in determining whether employees feel vital and energized at work, or if they feel depleted and exhausted instead.

Leaders Are the Key to Driving Workplace Wellness

Leaders in modern organizations are put under extreme pressure to drive the bottom line and shareholder value. At times, it can seem like that's the only thing that organizations want leaders to achieve. A report by Deloitte showed that 41 percent of leaders are stressed and 36 percent are exhausted.[1] Seventy percent of leaders don't even want to be leaders anymore because they are so unwell. At the same time, C-suites and boards are asking leaders to prioritize navigating uncertain economic conditions and strategically managing capital.[2] When leaders are already exhausted and stretched for time, it's no wonder that they often let employee wellness take a backseat to other, seemingly more important priorities.

At the heart of this conundrum is a simple fact: Most leaders view economic growth and financial management as being at odds with cultivating employee health and well-being. And they often believe they are already doing enough for employees. So, they push the responsibility for taking care of employees' wellness to their employer, hoping that a preexisting employee assistance program or a mindfulness session will fix the problem. But this approach is shortsighted. Indeed, organizations have also largely failed to crack the code on what promotes employee wellness at work. Most often, employers address employees' health and wellness through a set of perks or add-on initiatives that they believe signal that they care about employees' well-being. Currently, organizations are investing countless dollars in wellness solutions to align with employees' expectations and to help their employer brand stand out among competitors. These investments are becoming even more commonplace as new generations enter the workforce. Indeed, corporate wellness is an extremely large, and rapidly growing, industry. The global corporate wellness market was valued at $53 billion in 2022 and is expected to grow at a rate of 4.47% each year until 2030.[3] But is this money well spent?

The sad reality is that wellness-related metrics are not improving—rather, they are declining. The data suggests that employees are increasingly burned out. The dollars spent on wellness do not seem to be decreasing levels of exhaustion, stress, and burnout. Even companies that have invested heavily in wellness initiatives have struggled with a lack of results associated with those investments. More than half of U.S. workers report feeling exhausted and depleted of energy on the job, leading to extreme financial losses due to turnover and decreased productivity. In 2022, Gallup estimated the global cost of burnout to be $322 billion.[4] All of this data points to one bleak reality: Many organizations are failing to provide environments that help their employees to thrive. We argue that this is because wellness spending is being wasted on programs and initiatives that provide temporary solutions for persistent problems instead of preventing them from happening in the first place. If organizations want to attract, retain, and support happy, productive employees, they have to solve the puzzling gap between resources dedicated to wellness and their intended outcomes. Erroneously, many organizations assume this gap is an indicator that supporting employee health and wellness isn't profitable. This isn't the case— it's just that organizations have been focusing their time and money on the wrong solutions. Leaders are the heart of employee wellness, and they need to be developed appropriately to support their team's well-being while still boosting profits. When leaders recognize that their priorities of economic and financial growth are inherently linked with supporting employee health and wellness, they approach wellness strategically and from the top down.

When we talk to leaders working in companies struggling to support employee wellness, they often tell us they are trying more of the same: meditation programs for employees, step challenges, healthy cooking classes, or training on work-life balance strategies. These popular programs aren't inherently bad, but leaders also share that they don't seem to be fixing the problem. Leaders who truly consider what makes employees happy and healthy on the job aren't surprised to find out that popular wellness solutions fail to drive results. Yet searches for other remedies often leave these leaders empty-handed. A comprehensive employee wellness solution doesn't seem to exist. What should these leaders do?

We wondered the same thing. Now, in *Leading for Wellness*, we show you the answer. In short, leaders must go beyond the common, bottom-up solutions aimed at individual employees. We argue that these solutions tend to have limited impact because they ignore broader cultural and contextual features that are depleting wellness on a larger scale. In some instances, employers seem to blame employees for their wellness struggles, instead of taking ownership for creating a work environment that better supports employee thriving. This situation can be frustrating for employees because it can seem like companies are saying: "You aren't well? Take this course/

take part in this program/watch this webinar and learn how to get better at it. Good luck!" The elephant in the room is that leaders—at all levels—haven't taken a strategic approach to driving wellness from the top down. In this book, we shift the narrative by providing a research-based response to the question: How can leaders actually create a culture of wellness at work?

This book refocuses organizations away from wellness fads and trends and toward the building blocks of thriving workplace cultures—leaders. Most employees intuitively know what it feels like to work with a leader who helps them thrive—and what it feels like to work for a leader who does the opposite. Did you ever have a boss who sucked out all your energy, made your stress go through the roof, or who simply didn't take time to support your needs or desires as a person or employee? If so, did you ever think "When I become a leader, I'll do it differently"?

Many people believe that, when they become leaders, they'll be the one they would have wanted to work for in the past. Yet the number-one reason people leave their jobs is because they don't like their boss. So what happens? Why do people get off track when they become leaders? What gets in the way? Given the level of pressure to meet financial and business goals, plus the high levels of burn-out leaders themselves experience, leaders are easily derailed from becoming the stars they once dreamed they'd be. This book helps current and aspiring leaders, like you, to become the leader they've always wanted to work for—while still producing results and boosting their own well-being in the process.

Our Research

Why should you listen to us? We are two PhDs in industrial-organizational psychology with deep expertise in research and practice on workplace wellness and decades of combined experience in academia and industry. We have a passion for achieving workplace wellness in organizations, using straightforward, science-based practices, which have helped improve over 60 different organizations across diverse employee populations. The research we detail in this book helps you move away from the traditional workplace wellness fads and toward strategies that really work.

We set out to conduct our own independent research to build a blueprint for leaders who want to get back on track—or start out on the right foot—to become the leaders they promised themselves they'd be. Because we are scientists by training and trade, the foundations of this book are rooted around two major studies we conducted with different methodologies. It's important for research to be replicated to prove a result is real—and that's what we did.

Listening to Employees with Great Leaders

To conduct our first study, we spent a year interviewing employees who wanted to share their incredible experiences working with top leaders who created healthy and successful work environments. These interviews resulted in thousands of pages of data that we rigorously coded and analyzed to develop our framework for leading for wellness. We decided interviews would be the foundation for our study because they allowed us to gather rich, nuanced data about what leaders are doing to support wellness, the context they are deploying these actions within, and the impacts their actions are having on followers.

We were thoughtful about how we recruited interviewees. We wanted to ensure that leaders were not self-nominating for the study as being exemplary at supporting others' wellness. We can all name leaders who think they are great but whose employees disagree. Instead, we interviewed people who told us they reported to a leader who had supported their wellness. By interviewing the employees, instead of the leaders themselves, we avoided interviewing individuals who merely thought they were good at supporting the wellness of their team members. To recruit participants, we posted on various social media networks and asked participants to nominate other folks who also had worked with exemplary leaders.

Overall, we interviewed 50 participants before reaching saturation. *Saturation* is a technical term meaning the point at which we began hearing mostly repeating ideas and new insights stopped emerging. People's jobs varied significantly, ranging from junior roles all the way up to the C-suite. Study participants often described more than one leader who supported their wellness as part of the interview process. The companies that the participants and their leaders worked within spanned industries and organizational sizes. For example, we talked to people who were in HR-focused startups as well as to those working in financial services firms with over 300,000 employees. Our interviews led to thousands of pages of notes, full of stories and rich examples of good and bad leader behaviors. We systematically looked for themes across our notes, stories, and examples to pull out the key, consistent insights that our participants shared with us.

Replication Is Key

But we didn't stop there. We conducted our second study to ensure we could replicate our findings—an important part of good science. We utilized a survey of hundreds of employees this time, which led to thousands of unique insights that solidified our framework. Similar to the method we followed using our interview data, we extracted the most commonly occurring themes our participants shared and synthesized them into clear takeaways, rooted in their collective insights. All this research resulted in a guide for helping you to become a "Generator"—the type of leader whom people want to work for, that organizations want to hire, and that we hope you can ultimately say you are proud to be. We also help you avoid becoming an "Extinguisher"—the type of leader most employees swear they'll never become. Finally, we help you to recognize the personal benefits of being a Generator—namely, that it will decrease your own stress and burnout.

Results: Generators Support Employee Wellness Every Day

From our rigorous research, we find that leaders can build thriving, and more productive, workforces when they invest in supporting employee wellness at the source. Contrary to popular beliefs and large investments from companies, perks like wellness classes, resilience training, and healthy lifestyle initiatives (i.e., eating programs and step challenges) were not perceived as being the most helpful solutions for improving employee wellness. In fact, as mentioned, some employees even find them demeaning—as if their wellness challenges were being blamed on their own behaviors, without any consideration for the organizational environment they were working within. As Kassie, one of our participants, shared:

> We have a Wellness Committee and they put on events from time to time, and sometimes it's a guided meditation or whatever it is. But there's a little bit of irony because the only people that have the time to attend those [sessions] are the ones who are not as overworked and stressed out.

Instead, we find that employees view their day-to-day experiences with Generators and their team members as key determinants of wellness. They are seeking positive and healthy interactions at work to support their wellness, not a program or trendy benefit offering. We found that leaders who support employees' well-being are the biggest factor in determining if employee wellness needs are met and in boosting their productivity.

But beyond highlighting the fact that Generators drive employee and organizational success, this book provides you with clear guidelines for how you can become a Generator yourself. Our knowledge of the scientific literature, combined with our understanding of the realities organizations face in trying to shift cultures and leadership practices, led us to recognize that our research wouldn't stick with readers without a clear, actionable pathway toward becoming a Generator while steering clear of the trappings of Extinguishers. Our scientific approach to uncovering the key to generating workplace wellness provides easy steps for you to get started on improving your employees' health and well-being while still adding value to your organization and to your own life.

What Is Workplace Wellness?

We believe it's important for us to quickly clarify what we mean by "wellness" before we dig into the framework in more depth. The term "wellness" is used so broadly today that we all may be thinking of something different when using this word. For this reason, we asked employees themselves what they mean when they seek wellness at work. Without knowing what they want, how can we truly deliver?

In our research, we found that wellness is characterized by four main facets: physical health, mental health, emotional health, and work-life balance. When employees talked about physical health, they mentioned things like having time to exercise, maintaining good blood pressure markers, and getting the medical care they need. When discussing mental health, employees mentioned wanting support to take mental health days, access to mental health providers, and safety to discuss mental health challenges. Employees who mentioned emotional health prioritized receiving support to reduce stress and prevent burnout. They also wanted to experience greater feelings of energy and positivity at work. Finally, in terms of work-life balance, employees discussed receiving support for tackling work and life challenges, such as having time for their personal life and themselves, being able to prioritize family when needed, and being treated as whole people with many facets to their lives.

Importantly, our study participants felt that it wasn't enough to focus on just one of these four areas. Instead, they told us that it was important to think about wellness holistically. The phrase "considering the whole person" came up again and again in our interviews. For example, Chris, an HR leader, said: "I think workplace wellness definitely should support whole-person wellness." Sofia, an employee of a large healthcare organization, put it really well, saying,

> I think that I define [wellness] as an environment that is supported by [wellness-focused] policies and management that support the person's total health. So the physical environment, but also the company's culture and policies and, most importantly, leadership that supports total health. . .meaning mind, body, and spirit, but also your life outside of work.

Supporting employees' total health may seem like a tall order for leaders to deliver on—but we found it was possible, and easier than you might think.

Throughout this book, we use this holistic approach to wellness. Where noteworthy, we indicate if a specific component of wellness is more strongly impacted by certain behaviors. However, the behaviors and mindsets of leaders who support wellness generally impact the whole person, not just one dimension.

What to Expect from This Book

The beginning of our book sets the stage for you to prepare to increase your capacity to become a Generator. First, in Chapter 1, we provide a primer on the importance of wellness at work, and why it has such positive impacts on employees, leaders, organizations, and society. We put a special emphasis on the performance- and productivity-related benefits of becoming a more wellness-focused leader or organization.

Next, Part I of our book sets the stage for you to prepare to increase your capacity to become a Generator—a set of behaviors that shows the leader is a real person, with weaknesses and insecurities, and not a superhero. We discuss specific behaviors and strategies that you can deploy to enact the two core components of this pillar—firing your "work self" and embracing a struggle statement. Counterintuitively, we find that leaders who show their true, flawed selves support employee wellness far better than those who try to project an image of perfection.

In Part II, we take a deep dive into the second pillar of becoming a Generator—focusing on the tone being set, as opposed to the time being spent, at work. We then detail the two key dimensions of this pillar—setting the right tone and swiftly becoming a confidant. Most leaders believe that the hours they put in are directly related to the results they get out, but we change the narrative by showing that the way things are done is more important than the time spent doing them.

In Part III, we cover the next core component of being a Generator—crafting work to support life, instead of squeezing your life in around your work. Here we teach you how to improve your elasticity in responding to employees' unique needs and desires. We also show you how to become a "boundary bouncer"—someone who helps employees set and enforce healthy boundaries between work and life. Even staunch supporters of work-life balance usually believe that, when push comes to shove, work comes first. We show how Generators uniquely and wisely promote the opposite.

In Part IV, we cover the final component of being a Generator—recognizing that supporting employee wellness isn't one-size-fits-all. Here we show you how to engage in a process of person-centered planning with your team members and discuss how you can destigmatize mental health challenges that your employees may be facing. Employee wellness programs usually offer the same set of benefits to all employees, without consideration for their specific struggles. Generators recognize the need to tailor wellness strategies to each employee, and they do so successfully.

In all four of these parts, we get very granular about the specific actions that you can take to ensure you are becoming more like the Generators we spotlight and less like the Extinguishers who zap employees' energy and motivation. We share stories from our research and de-identified quotes from our participants. While we edited our quotes for clarity, all of the stories are real. We also provide reflections, activities, and worksheets for you to complete at the end of each chapter (with the exclusion of Chapter 1), so that you can start applying your learnings right away.

In Part V, we discuss challenges and barriers that you may face on your journey toward becoming a Generator as well as strategies for overcoming these roadblocks. Here we also provide tools for you to create concrete action plans for improving your Generator leadership capabilities and for diminishing tendencies toward Extinguisher behaviors. Overall, after reading this book, you will be able to anticipate and plan for setbacks in your journey toward becoming a Generator and have an action plan that will set your wheels in motion immediately.

By following our guidance, you can become the leader you've always dreamed of working for. Importantly, you will also be able to promote employee wellness, and boost performance and productivity, in a healthy and sustainable way. Instead of providing a series of stand-alone suggestions for initiatives (e.g., mindfulness meditation, yoga at lunch, etc.), we provide a behavioral guide that shows you exactly how to become an exemplary people leader, using tips that anyone can follow—no matter your career stage, size of your organization, your industry, or your financial resources. By the end of the book, we know you'll be motivated and prepared to take the right actions to become a Generator at work. Let's start Generating!

Key Takeaways

- Traditional workplace wellness programs (e.g., mindfulness, healthy eating initiatives, etc.) do not solve the root problems of burnout.

- These workplace wellness programs are often costly and, unfortunately, do not drive productivity and results alone.

- Employees view leaders as having the greatest day-to-day impact on their wellness.

- The actions and behaviors outlined in this book are based on insights derived from rigorous and replicated research that produced a framework for becoming a Generator leader and for avoiding becoming an Extinguisher leader.

- Generators allow employees to thrive and reach their full potential; Extinguishers exhaust employees and put barriers on their paths to goal achievement.

- You can become a Generator. This book will show you how.

Chapter 1

Why Workplace Wellness Matters

When I was under her [leadership], I definitely felt more engaged with my work. I felt more excited about the job that I was doing and I wanted to put in a ton of effort for her.
　　　　　　—Jelisa, supply chain employee, study participant

If you are reading this book, it's unlikely that you need convincing that workplace wellness is important. Unfortunately, many senior executives see business and wellness as completely separate. In their view, it is not the responsibility of the business or of leadership to take care of employee well-being. Instead, getting employees to work longer and harder is the goal, regardless of the consequences to their health and happiness. Even leaders who want to support their employees' wellness often think that doing so is a pure cost to the business, instead of a gain. One of the most dangerous trends we have seen is when companies pretend that they care about wellness by offering programs or initiatives that actually keep employees at work longer and make them feel more obligated to be always available. For example, it's great if your company offers free meals in a cafeteria. But that also encourages employees to eat all of their meals—including breakfast and dinner—at work. The outcome of these seemingly benevolent workplace wellness programs is burnout or disenchantment. Companies that engage in this form of performative workplace well-being don't understand that spending money on programs like these leads to even more money lost in the long run. Instead, ensuring leaders understand that demonstrating a genuine concern for wellness is what matters—both for employees and for driving business results. So, in this chapter, we want to help you convince those around you that workplace wellness is worth focusing on.

Wellness Affects Everyone

To give you clear direction, we discuss the importance of wellness from four different perspectives:

1. For employees, we highlight research that shows how healthy and well mental states promote efficiency and performance at work.

2. Leaders might also support health and wellness for slightly selfish reasons. We think that getting leaders to the table to support workplace wellness is an important first step, regardless of the reason why they initially take that step. Therefore, if you need to convince leaders to care about employee wellness because there is something in it for them, that's better than not having convinced them at all. Over time, as leaders see the positive impact of leading for wellness, we hope they grow their capacity to lead in this way for more altruistic reasons. But if your leaders aren't there yet, focusing on the leadership benefits may be a good starting point. The good news is that research clearly shows that leaders themselves can benefit from creating a healthier environment for their employees by experiencing higher goal achievement, stronger relationships, and increased effectiveness and productivity.

3. We show how companies benefit from an intentional focus on wellness by seeing improvements in their bottom line. This is another less altruistic reason for increasing your capacity to lead for wellness (i.e., caring about employee wellness because it is profitable). But it's still a great entry point into the conversation if that's the most effective way to capture your leader's attention.

4. Finally, organizations have broad implications for our society and economy. The reason we are passionate about workplace wellness is because we believe companies can harness their power for societal good more effectively. If companies are producing employees who are feeling whole, vigorous, and excited about their work and lives (on average; everyone has tough days sometimes no matter what), workers can give back to their communities, their families, and themselves much more fully. In contrast, when employees are burned out, saddled with stress, and feeling emotionally taxed, they don't have the same energy to give to make the world a better place.

In other words, when companies offer more vibrant and fulfilling places to work, our communities share in that vibrancy and fulfillment. We think that's reason enough to care about workplace wellness, but in case your leaders disagree, next we unpack the first three reasons to help you make the case instead.

The Impact of Wellness on Employees

Think about a time when you were super productive and doing your best at work. Take a moment to imagine how you were feeling. What was the situation? What was the work environment like? What did your leader do, if anything, to help you get to this point? Now think about your life outside of work during that time. How was your sleep? What was going on in your personal life? How was your physical health? How was your mental and emotional health?

Relish in that memory for a minute, pause, and now think about a different time, a time when you were not feeling productive or effective at work. How were you feeling? What was the work environment like? Did your leader contribute to your inability to be productive? Now think about your life outside of work. Were you getting enough restful sleep? Were you able to disconnect from work? How was your health and wellness overall?

Take a moment to consider the differences between these two reflections. We guess that reflecting on the first scenario makes you feel much more positive than reflecting on the second one does. It might even be painful to reflect on the second scenario in many ways. Think about living the first scenario over and over, compared to living the second scenario over and over. Your work experiences can accumulate over time to impact your work and life—for better or worse. This is why working in a consistently positive work environment makes such a big positive impact on employee well-being. Having a really bad day every now and then is manageable; having a really bad day most of the time is not.

In this exercise, you may have noticed a link between how you were feeling and the level of productivity you were able to achieve. We all know how challenging it is to work when you are really tired, overly stressed, or feeling sick. And if work is the reason why you feel unwell, being productive is even harder. It takes longer to get basic tasks done. It's hard to come up with new ideas or solutions to challenges. And it's more likely that you'll take negative emotions out on your coworkers in ways that might damage your social relationships. When you take a moment to think about it, it's clear that you can't be your best when you aren't feeling your best.

Thus, it is apparent that wellness can have a huge impact on employee performance, productivity, and effectiveness. The research supports this finding. Abundant scientific evidence shows that employees who are more well also perform better. As the amount of research is extensive, we will highlight some of the key findings here.

More Satisfied Employees Are More Productive

A large body of research shows the importance of employees feeling a sense of satisfaction on the job. It's been well established that more satisfied employees are more productive.[1] Specifically, employees who feel good about the work itself, their coworkers, their company, and their manager are more likely to be effective on the job. Unfortunately, employees sometimes struggle to feel satisfied at work, especially when their wellness needs aren't met.[2] Even if employees have their dream jobs and are a great fit for all their role responsibilities, they may not always end up healthy and happy in the long run. When employees are working unsustainable hours or they are working in a toxic work environment (or both), burnout can occur. Burnout can quickly derail employees in any type of job (dream jobs included!) and cause them to feel negatively about the people they work with or their overall work experience.[3] For example, employees experiencing burnout are more likely to resent their managers, their peers, the company, and even the job itself. So even employees who started out happy on the job may become disgruntled over time. This finding is critical because burned-out employees perform worse than their more energized colleagues. Thus, boosting wellness decreases burnout, which impacts employees' ability to perform on the job.[4] Ensuring that employees are not overworked, overwhelmed, or exhausted helps employees and organizations alike.

Employee Wellness Boosts Engagement

Research also shows that boosting employee wellness usually leads to increased employee engagement.[5] Most leadership teams understand the importance of keeping employees engaged. Likely you've taken an employee experience survey. Surveys are common ways leaders seek to understand employee engagement and inform possible solutions to improve it. Employees who are engaged can enter a state of "flow."[6] Flow occurs when employees feel energized and motivated to continue working hard at their jobs. When employees are in flow, their hard work doesn't translate into burnout. Instead, they become more energized and motivated, which helps boost their productivity. In contrast, employees who are experiencing burnout are likely to disengage from their work and their organizations.[7] Employees whose energy is depleted lose focus more easily and are more sluggish on the job and in completing work tasks. Even if the task is normally enjoyable, it's hard for employees who lack basic energy to find their flow. Although leaders understand the importance of engagement, they often overlook the powerful solution of supporting employee wellness. The research in this area is quite clear—focusing on employee wellness boosts employee engagement. Leaders cannot ignore the wellness part of this equation if they want to see employee engagement improve.

Wellness Improves Employee Commitment

Further, employee wellness is also related to improved employee commitment.[8] When employees are committed to their leaders in particular, they want to show up and put more time and effort into their work.[9] Rochelle, a consultant for a global software company, noted:

I get more done [under my wellness-focused leader]....I think there is an element of want[ing] to get things done, not just because it's your job, but because you want to do well for your team, for the product. So, it's some intrinsic motivation too.

Just as with engagement, employees who put in extra time and effort because they want to and because they have the energy to do so have a lower risk of burnout. Thus, increasing employee commitment is a positive conduit to driving results.

However, employees in companies that struggle to support their wellness are less likely to feel committed at work. As you may expect, when employees feel less committed to their work, they tend to perform worse and are more likely to want to leave their jobs.[10] They are also more likely to engage in what is now known as quiet quitting. They display what researchers call *withdrawal behaviors*, decreasing their investment and psychological connection to their work, even though they are still present on the job.[11] The bottom line is that employees do their best work when they care enough to put in the time and energy. From an employee perspective, caring about your work can feel a lot better than the opposite. Supporting employee wellness is a key way to cultivate caring in employees.

In sum, employees are more satisfied, more engaged in their work, and more committed to their organizations when their wellness needs are met. Nia, an HR employee at a small startup, shared: "Being happy at work keeps us more productive and more engaged. It just follows—you could be having a bad day at home and then go to work, and your day turns around." In turn, when employees are feeling better at work, they are more productive and perform at higher levels. Thus, investing in employee wellness is a win for everyone. More on that next.

Leaders Benefit from Well Employees

If there's one thing we learned from our research on how to be a Generator, or a leader who supports employees' wellness, it's that great leaders truly care about their employees as whole people. Yet they aren't overly idealistic either. These leaders are also good stewards of their companies and work hard to ensure the business does well. Unfortunately, not all leaders are like the Generators we learned about. To contrast with the exemplary leaders they wanted to discuss with us, many participants shared examples of Extinguishers who didn't care about or consider their employees' well-being. But even leaders who don't care about others probably do care about themselves. Thus, to help bring these leaders along on the journey, it's important to understand how they themselves might benefit from improving employee wellness. Plus, we assume that you're reading this book because you'd like to become a Generator. Even if your motivations are geared more toward others than yourself, it's still nice to know what's in it for you from a leadership perspective. Luckily, the plethora of research on workplace wellness shows that leaders do benefit from a focus on employee well-being.

Generators Enjoy Strong Relationships with Employees

Strong leader relationships and employee wellness have been shown to go hand in hand.[12] Maybe some leaders don't think building strong relationships with employees is worth the time. That's a shortsighted conclusion. Although supporting employees' wellness may take time, the relational benefits are clear—and outweigh the risks of having poor relationships with your direct reports. Employees are much more likely to be dedicated and committed to their leader when that person supports their wellness.[13] We already talked about commitment leading to better performance. Thus, supportive leaders likely have higher-performing teams, and these teams make the leaders look good. In other words, having more dedicated employees boosts performance, which generally brings positive recognition to the leader from across the organization.

But, beyond improving overall performance, dedicated and committed employees are more likely to stay on the team. This finding may have positive implications for leaders who depend on their team to work closely with them over an extended period or who would suffer from knowledge or skills gaps if valuable employees left. In other words, if you want team members to stick by you through challenges, take initial steps to stick by them. When employees know their leader truly cares about them and other team members, they are more appreciative and grateful for the leader.[14] And leaders who boost their employees' wellness also benefit from having a positive reputation across the organization. Increased appreciation and gratitude, in turn, can facilitate positive social interactions and a sense of reciprocity and generosity. Workplaces in which leaders have similarly strong relationships with all of their team members are more enjoyable, connected, and fun for everyone—including the leader.[15]

Generators Have More Creative and Innovative Teams

Leaders who support their employees' wellness also benefit from enhanced team innovation and creativity.[16] More innovative and creative teams can work smarter rather than working longer and harder. The reason is that, when employees feel supported, they are more likely to bring up new ideas on how to improve work products, services, or processes.[17] Further, healthier and happier teams not only come up with more creative ideas for improving deliverables, they also come up with new and valuable ways to improve how they work together. Imagine having a team that is known across the company as innovative, collaborative, and efficient. Leading a team that consistently thinks up valuable new ideas and that positively models collaboration and teamwork shines a positive light on the leader.

Leaders of these teams may be top of mind when new opportunities arise for expanding their leadership (e.g., promotions, stretch projects). For this reason, leaders who support their employees' wellness may also progress in their careers more quickly and easily.

Generators and Their Teams Achieve Goals

Finally, leaders are expected to drive progress toward and achieve key business goals. If a leader supports employee wellness, employees are more likely to achieve their goals.[18] Employee goal achievement helps the leader meet their objectives as well—especially since most corporate environments include cascaded goals. As mentioned earlier, when employees are energized and engaged with their work, they perform better. Leaders are only as good as their teams. Even more appealing to leaders is the fact that when employees perform better, the leader's job becomes easier. Leaders of high-performing teams are freed up to focus on more strategic work and to spend more time influencing their own senior leadership. This situation might have a snowball effect, such that these leaders of high-performing teams can become increasingly more impactful as a function of their team's increased wellness.

We hope you are reading this book because you care about your employees and about making a positive impact as a leader, but note that you can reap concrete benefits by supporting employee wellbeing. By leading for wellness, you can build a positive workplace where people are truly connected in their quest toward success. Your team will be committed to helping you and will be more successful in achieving goals together. And your team will be more innovative and creative, producing high-quality work in more efficient and effective ways. After this chapter, we give you the precise tools you need to be a Generator who can drive these amazing results. For now, let's consider some other reasons that leading for wellness is important.

Wellness Boosts the Bottom Line

So far, we've talked about the personal impact of wellness on employees and leaders. However, we know that the bottom line typically drives decisions within organizations. As you may anticipate based on all the benefits described earlier, organizations that support employee wellness typically are higher performing.[19] When employees are happy and healthy, they perform better. If you extrapolate this out to the organization level, the bottom line improves when there are many happy and healthy employees and productive teams.[20]

> When employees are happier and healthier, companies can attract and retain the best and brightest employees.

The opposite is true too. When employees experience burnout and struggle with their wellness, the organization's financial bottom line suffers.[21] Employees who aren't well disengage, quiet quit, produce less, use more sick days, and eventually leave.[22] All of these counterproductive work behaviors can cost companies huge amounts of money. Gallup estimates that something as common as disengagement costs the world $8.8 trillion in lost productivity.[23] Turnover is estimated to cost from half to two times an employee's annual salary.[24] These two examples alone show the staggering financial impact of employee struggles with wellness. Laney, now a regional director for a national educational organization, left her previous job because of a lack of wellness-focused leadership. She summed up the sentiment we are describing: "The mental stress [of my job] was really never addressed, and that's been the bigger issue and was one of the reasons why I left. Because the workload continued to grow and the support was not there."

Finally, organizations that support employee wellness tend to be viewed more favorably by the general public, which improves business by attracting more customers and contributing to a strong employee value proposition. In other words, organizations that ensure employees are happier and healthier can attract and retain the best and the brightest employees.[25] Everyone wants to work for an employer that cares about them. Kassie, the senior leader at a boutique consulting firm mentioned in the introduction, shared: "I've been stressed out and challenged many times [at work]. But I stayed because I felt supported and I felt like I had a partner in problem-solving [with my leader]." Plus, prospective employees usually look for employment opportunities where they anticipate they'll be happy and able to achieve work-life balance. If an organization has a repu-tation as a great place to work, candidates will gravitate toward it. And, once there, employees will be less likely to leave. It's hard to leave a workplace where you are treated well and able to thrive. Thus, workplaces that focus on improving employee wellness can attract and retain employees longer and may cultivate a more positive public reputation as a result. Overall, focusing on employee wellness can support organizational profitability and revenue growth. Putting in the effort to develop a team of Generators will be worth it. Your Chief Financial Officer (CFO) will thank you (and if you're the CFO, you'll thank yourself).

Societal Implications of Employee Wellness

Finally, we want to acknowledge the broader societal implications of improving workplace wellness. When we started Workr Beeing, we were motivated by a deep understanding of the massive impact organizations can have on society at large. Increasing the focus of organizations on employee wellness will impact the vitality of our communities and the world as a whole. We believe organizations have a responsibility to the communities they are located within, the regions they serve, and the people whose lives they touch.

Workr Beeing (workrbeeing.com) is our business and brand. We leverage our workplace wellness expertise to help organizations build thriving workplaces. We deliver keynotes, participate in speaking engagements, conduct workshops, develop executives, and provide accessible content to help organizations create positive work environments. We also co-host the "Thriving at Work" podcast, sharing research and tips for improving workplace wellness.

For example, burnout and work-related stress doesn't stay at work. Burned-out, tired, and frustrated employees bring that negative energy home to their friends and family.[26] When we have asked our clients and students about the first thing they do after a bad day at work, the number-one answer is always that they talk about it with family or friends. (Drinking alcohol is also a common answer.) In other words, employees are likely to vent about their work challenges to those closest to them.[27] Unfortunately, emotions—especially negative ones—are contagious, and the misery can spread to those outside of the organization. Not only will employees be less satisfied with their personal lives based on their bad experiences at work, but so will those closest to them. This type of stress and burnout can stifle positive relationships and home environments.

Senior leaders do care about more than the bottom line. In fact, when we ask senior leaders to contemplate their impact on the world, we also tell them about the impact that negative workplace experiences can have on employees and those they love. We have witnessed many lightbulb moments where executives begin to realize that their impact on the world starts with the employees in their organization but spills over to folks outside as well. Most leaders don't want to hurt their employees, their employees' significant others, children, or friends. Indeed, they often openly share their goals to support employees' health and well-being. Many have experienced relational or health challenges themselves and know how hard it can be to manage work and life at the same time. Yet if they don't take employee wellness seriously, their fears of putting more harm into the world than good may be realized, even inadvertently. Often this reality is motivating enough for them to stop engaging in some negative behaviors. We hope that your leaders will feel the same.

In contrast, when employees have a positive and fulfilling work life, the people around them will also have happier and healthier lives. And they will be able to enjoy each other's company in higher-quality ways and for longer. In fact, decreased work stress is related to longevity.[28] Asher, a leader at a tech startup who was diagnosed with late-stage cancer, shared that having a wellness-focused leader truly had life-or-death consequences. He said: "I was diagnosed with pancreatic cancer. And this company, because of the practices they have engaged in, I feel is a huge part of why I'm going to be okay. I attribute a lot of the reason that I'm recovering [to] them." Wouldn't it be great if instead of harming employees and their communities, your company contributed to the thriving and longevity of those who contribute to the company's well-being? Returning to our earlier discussion of wellness-focused leadership decreasing the likelihood of turnover, Asher also shared that his leader's care and grace while he was going through cancer treatment made him a loyal employee for life. He stated: "I've told [my boss], 'Another company could offer me double my salary and I'd turn it down in a heartbeat without a second thought.'" That's the power of leading for wellness.

In addition, when employees are less depleted and more energized, they are more likely to give back to their communities.[29] When employees feel taken care of as human beings, they take action to improve humanity. That action may be through volunteerism to help improve the lives of others around them or by taking time to help a family member, neighbor, or friend. In other words, taking good care of employees has ripple effects. Organizations that support employee

14

Leading for Wellness

wellness can have a broader reach to create more caring communities and, it is hoped, a more caring world.

We believe organizations need to take the impact that they have on the world seriously. Some organizations focus on corporate social responsibility and the sustainability of our physical environment. But what about the sustainability of the employees—the people who do the work to make companies succeed? If all organizations tried to take steps to improve their employees' wellness, think about how much more energy and positivity would be infused in our neighborhoods, communities, and nations.

Overall, the focus of this book is on creating well, thriving work environments through the power of leading for wellness. There are so many reasons to take care of others in the workplace. As a leader, we hope you take your responsibility seriously and influence those around you to do the same. More important, we hope that this chapter has given you the tools you need to convince key decision makers in your organization (or yourself) that focusing on leading for wellness is crucial for improving employees' work and lives, for boosting the bottom line in a sustainable way, and for making the world a better place.

Key Takeaways

- Supporting employee wellness leads to healthier employees who perform better, achieve their goals, and are more committed to their work.

- When leaders support employee wellness, their employees are more committed to them and the team. They help

(Continued)

(Continued)

leaders achieve goals, build a creative and innovative work environment, and band together when facing challenges.

- Organizations can benefit from a focus on employee wellness. Employee wellness boosts profitability.

- Caring for employee wellness can have a broader impact beyond the walls of the organization. Happy, healthy employees bring positivity to their communities, making the world a better place.

Part I

No One Wants a Superhero

It's time to dig into the behaviors of Generators and learn how you can become one. In this part, we outline the first core set of behaviors that Generators engage in—showing that they are real human beings who are vulnerable, who have weaknesses, and who need help from others. In other words, we reveal that Generators recognize that their followers don't want a superhero. Instead, they want someone they can aspire to be like, without having to lose who they truly are in the process. We detail the two main sets of Generator behaviors that show that they are human beings and not superhuman—firing their work self and embracing their struggle statement.

Chapter 2

Fire Your Work Self

For better or worse, [my boss] is very forthcoming about his own life, and so, it made it pretty easy for me to be as forthcoming about what was going on with mine. So, in that sense, it was actually as easy as it can be to have that conversation [about my parent's health struggles].

—Monica, data analyst, study participant

Melanie is a high-ranking leader at a large telecommunications company who was described as always having her game face on. When we interviewed her for our research, she explained how prior leaders at other companies had shaped her leadership style. Melanie admitted to starting out as a no-nonsense leader. She was a solid rock during times of stress, ready for any challenge that came her team's way. Melanie believed that her team would find comfort in her tough exterior. If she couldn't face every challenge head on without fear, how could others muster the courage to do so? However, in the long term, she found that her demeanor caused more problems than it provided solutions. Melanie learned that if her team members were struggling with something—anything— they did not want to flag it up to her. Instead of feeling comfortable raising concerns or issues with her, they feared that Melanie would see them as ineffective or incapable. They all thought that when Melanie faced challenges, she was able to overcome them effortlessly and without help from others. Melanie's tough and "perfect" exterior made her seem unapproachable rather than an ideal leader.

Perfectionists Are Unapproachable

This "perfect" exterior posed a problem for team members and became an issue for Melanie herself. While the team viewed Melanie as a stone-faced leader who was never ruffled by challenges, unbeknownst to them, she was struggling with something that her team couldn't see. Her family was going through an unspeakable tragedy—her youngest sibling had been murdered in a random act of violence only weeks before. Instead of sharing her struggles with the team, however, she tried to do what she always did—push through the emotions and hide them from the world. However, given these more extreme circumstances, Melanie told us that the team noticed something was off. As you can imagine, Melanie was falling apart after her unexpected and senseless loss. But although team members recognized that Melanie seemed slightly different from her usual self, no one felt comfortable talking about what was going on—least of all Melanie.

However, everything changed when Melanie started to learn from the leaders above her. She talked about an initiative that helped her open up:

> There was a campaign [about admitting you're struggling with mental health] that was launched [around the same time], just to really further emphasize that it's okay to not always be positive about things, or it's okay to not always be in a happy-go-lucky mood, and that sometimes we all struggle and that's a part of the human condition. So that's been really heartwarming for me personally, but then to

also hear from other people who have gone through challenges from a mental health and mental illness perspective and finding the right resources and being on a path toward wellness has been just incredibly enriching for me to experience personally.

When Melanie started seeing her leaders sharing their personal experiences and stories, she was able to view them in a different light—as whole, complex people. She began to wonder if she should do the same.

A few weeks later, as she led her team through a routine meeting, a team member brought up an issue with one of their strategies for achieving a team goal. If true, the issue would set the team back from making progress on an important project. For Melanie, this was the last thing she could handle amid her personal struggles. However, this time, instead of characteristically ignoring and hiding her feelings, Melanie decided to pause the meeting and to share her struggles. She let her team know that she was on the verge of being overwhelmed and overworked and that her response was not due to the team or their productivity. In fact, she was grateful for their hard work. Instead, she told them the truth behind her reaction. She told them about the sudden and horrific circumstances of her sibling's death. She shared that she and her family were stricken with grief and unresolved anger. Melanie even shared her personal emotional struggles, including that she was spending most of her nights at home crying or trying to sleep away the pain. She shared that she tried to keep her personal trauma from the team to keep up the persona that she could handle anything at any time, no matter what. Finally becoming her authentic self, Melanie shared that it was too challenging to be a seemingly "perfect" person in the long term. Her hardships were zapping her of the energy and strength she needed to persist through work challenges.

After sharing such personal and difficult insights, Melanie looked up hesitantly to see the team's reaction. As she described it, a sense of compassion, empathy, and care swept the room. The team all jumped in with their condolences and started offering ways to help. They asked if they could cover some of Melanie's work tasks and how they could provide emotional support. In the short term, the team rallied around her, relieved that she was finally able to be real with them.

Eventually Melanie also sensed a longer-term shift in the team's energy. Namely, the team embraced their no-longer "perfect" leader. They finally knew it was okay to have flaws too. After that moment, Melanie's team was much more forthcoming about their own struggles, work related or not. She benefited from the support and help from her direct reports and ultimately received more frequent and useful information from her team. The team grew a lot closer, their well-being improved, and they were more dedicated to working for and with Melanie than before.

Melanie credits her ability to become her authentic self to the leaders around her who shared their personal stories, struggles, and journeys. She mentioned that the COVID-19 pandemic helped those leaders become more vulnerable. Their vulnerability really impacted her. As she reflected on her leadership style prior to the pandemic, she shared:

All of those things happening created an opportunity to more genuinely express what you were going through. And I know, at least for me personally, I had never gotten to such a state of—I don't know if I will call it burnout— but of feeling unwell before that point. And so I think for me it was harder to even relate. And I look back on it, and if people on my team were struggling in that, I probably could have been labeled as a toxic positive boss. Because it was always happy and [saying] "Everything's good!"

In sum, Melanie eventually recognized the positive aspects of becoming an authentic leader. She got the support she needed, built better relationships with her team, and was able to drive the team's success more effectively. Melanie's experience helped her become the Generator her team ultimately needed.

Professional Norms Hold Leaders Back

As Melanie's story shows, it's normal for people to act differently at work compared to how they act in their personal lives. In fact, sometimes professional norms can be helpful. They provide a road-map for how to behave in ways that others read as businesslike. These norms ensure that people are held accountable for inappropriate behavior at work. But can these norms go too far? At what point are norms doing more than just discouraging bad behavior but also discouraging people from showing some of what makes them real people? Melanie is a great example of a leader who made a big change toward authenticity after a time of trauma. We hope you won't have to experience such a difficult time before you make this type of change. Instead, we hope that this book will help you shift toward becoming a Generator without experiencing pain and struggle first.

In a post-COVID-19 world, employees worldwide have come to recognize that everyone faces challenges sometimes—even leaders. As the pandemic unfolded, employees and leaders alike experienced their share of work-related and other existential crises. Struggles with mental health, work-family conflict, social isolation, and loneliness ran rampant. Loneliness combined with the common experience of the pandemic helped many employees and leaders share their authentic selves at work in ways that were unheard of before. Receiving support, encouragement, and consideration from leaders in response to the authentic struggles that employees share can build stronger, more trusting relationships.[1] For employees who experienced these strengthened connections with their leaders, there is no going back.

Unfortunately, long-standing norms for leaders did not evolve as quickly during and after the pandemic as the experience and expectations of the broader employee base. Most of our norms for professionalism come from watching leaders who are held up as role models in our organizations and in society. For years, these role models were buttoned-up, top-down, authoritative leaders who embodied the "ideal worker" persona. The focus of their lives was work and everything else was a secondary concern or, worse, a distraction. Certainly, some shifts have happened in leadership norms recently. For example, tech leaders have paved the way for a more laidback dress code at work, changing the expectation of how leaders present themselves. But these changes are slow, and many traditional ideas about leadership still prevail. One of the longest-standing norms for leaders is extremely difficult to shake—the norm that leaders must appear unwaveringly productive in the face of challenges. Under the guidance of this norm, leaders are viewed as fearless problem solvers, helping to shepherd employees through challenging times, often without acknowledging their own struggles.

Thus, despite a broader awareness that employees are real people, the norms of what a leader should be continue. As a result, many leaders are trying to reenact the same old leadership scripts, even though the cast of characters surrounding them has changed significantly. There is an opportunity to update leadership behaviors to better align with employee expectations—if we can finally let go of our traditional norms expecting leaders to be uniform, endlessly efficient, and productive individuals.

Encouragingly, we also found that employees reject inauthentic, workaholic, one-track-minded leaders who expect them to fall in line with old professional norms. In fact, our participants shared that they *never* wanted these types of leaders and that the pandemic gave them a much-desired peek at what life could be like with an authentic leader.

Beyond Melanie's example, we found that many employees are seeking vulnerable leaders. They want leaders who show their teams who they really are—and that's exactly what Generators do. Generators show vulnerability through actions as simple as sharing stories about meaningful hobbies or as complex as confiding a worry or concern about their own abilities to succeed.

To become a Generator, you need to examine the gaps between the authentic version of yourself and the version of yourself that shows up at work. As Ralph Waldo Emerson once famously wrote: "To be yourself in a world that is constantly trying to make you something else is the greatest accomplishment." You need to uncover the "something else" you may have become at work, fire that inauthentic self, and start living and working in a way that is uniquely reflective of you—helping you become the Generator you are motivated to be. The "Take Action" section and the companion worksheet (Worksheet 2.1) at the end of this chapter are good starting points for becoming a more authentic leader at work.

Research Supports the Case for Authenticity

By now you know that, as scientists, we want to deeply understand the evidence and research that supports every recommended insight and action. And we want to share this research with you. Scientific evidence is useful for understanding the broader, data-driven impacts of people's actions at work. In addition to our own research findings, science has supported the benefits of authenticity, both in and out of work, for decades.

Despite norms for professionalism that encourage everyone to look and act similarly, authenticity is important for supporting high-quality relationships and productivity at work. For instance, research shows that when leaders express themselves authentically, their employees trust them more.[2] In fact, a recent experiment conducted by Anna Elisabeth Weischer, Jürgen Weibler, and Malte Petersen from the University of Hagen in Germany showed the powerful impact of leaders sharing stories with their teams.[3] In the study, participants were asked to read about leaders telling different types of stories. Some read about a leader who vividly recounted stories about personal, negative life events. Others read about a leader who shared more neutral life stories. Still others read about a leader who didn't share stories at all. Interestingly, participants had the best reaction to the leader who vividly shared the personal, negative stories. People trusted that leader more than the others because the leader was willing to get personal and vulnerable with them.

In the long term, employees' beliefs about the willingness of leaders to speak on difficult but important realities matter because these beliefs create trust between leaders and their team members. Trust is important between employees and their leaders, not only for the sake of the relationship, but also for the bottom line. Employees who trust their leaders actually perform better.[4] Trust is built when employees believe that their leader has their best interests at heart. Employees trust leaders they can rely on to provide solid advice and guidance when times are tough. Generators exhibited these behaviors in our research as well. Generators are dependable and reliable, and they consistently show authentic care and concern.

When employees believe that leaders are acting in their own self-interest or in inauthentic ways, they are likely to feel that their leaders are unpredictable and less trustworthy. People trust leaders whom they know well because they can predict how those leaders will act in particular situations. If employees are unsure about whether they know the "real" you, they struggle to anticipate your reaction, response, or behavior to various work contexts or scenarios. That inability to predict your behavior leads to lower levels of trust, which can weaken relationships with team members over time. Extinguishers are prime examples of leaders who are perceived as untrustworthy. Because they don't show their authentic selves to their teams, their employees struggle to fully trust and understand them.

Research also finds that leader authenticity leads to increased employee engagement.[5] When employees see their leader being open and honest, they feel the freedom to do the same. Such employees are more likely to express themselves on the job and add their personal flair to their work, a situation that can be extremely motivating for employees. We all like to see ourselves reflected in the work we do. As employees become more personally attached and invested in the way they do their work, they become more engaged with it.

Research shows that authentic leaders are more likely to discuss and share their "why" with followers.[6] They discuss what motivates them, what scares them, and what they are hoping to achieve. They make their "why" clear and often bring things back to their personal, authentic North Star. This behavior helps employees link to a greater sense of purpose in their work. Understanding their leader's "why" helps them find their own. And when employees feel more purpose in their work, they are more likely to become energized by and motivated to complete their tasks.[7] Thus, leader authenticity can increase employee productivity. Overall, leader authenticity is a huge win-win. Generators are fantastic role models of authenticity, encouraging employees to take steps toward authenticity themselves. We learned that employees appreciated feeling like their leader wanted to know them authentically. They felt supported to do their work in their unique way. They didn't feel the fear of judgment that often comes when a leader is not modeling authenticity.

Employees Want Authentic Leaders

Although research supports the importance of leaders being authentic, many leaders still present a "work self" on the job. You may do the same. If so, when and why do you feel pressure to act in ways that go against your real nature? Do you think there's a gap between your work self and your personal-life self? You will reflect on this further when you complete Worksheet 2.1.

In general, being open and honest about who you are can be scary. We fear judgment. The more you share of yourself, the more rejection or conflict can hurt. Staying closed off from others can be a good defense mechanism against rejection. However, it also shields you from having the joy of true connection and meaningful relationships with others. Relationships with colleagues are important. We spend so much time at work that missing out on those connections and wasting mental energy hiding your true self can harm your well-being.

Many leaders act inauthentically because they aren't sure how else to act. We often base our behaviors on our role models. Like Melanie, we use the leaders who have come before us as templates for how we should lead. Although this strategy is logical and natural, copying other leaders isn't helpful for breeding authenticity, and it can be extremely exhausting. And, as discussed earlier, employees suffer when their leader is inauthentic.

> Do you know why you haven't always been authentic at work? Understanding the reasons can help you on your journey to becoming a Generator. Take a moment to reflect. How authentic are you really? What stops you from being authentic? Are you afraid of judgment? Are you simply following others' examples without thinking about who you want to be as a leader?

Authenticity Can Be Simple

Our research findings reflect the trend that most leaders do not present their most authentic selves at work. Generators may be a less common type of leader in the workplace but they stand out as being particularly motivating, effective, and supportive of employee well-being. They are the shining example that, we hope, the next generation of leaders can follow to create healthier workplaces. And that change can start with your own journey to becoming a Generator. Let's take a look at a leader who didn't have to experience a traumatic event, like Melanie, to change her approach.

Carol has been a leader at her company for decades and is seen as being "all business" at work. But Carol has a secret. She has a passion for painting and always finds time in her personal life to engage in her passion as a creative outlet. Carol loves to paint nature scenes or flowers but, honestly, the object of the painting isn't what matters to her. It is the act of painting that makes Carol happy. She paints whenever she can, and her friends and family admire her dedication to her art.

Knowing what a central role Carol's passion plays in her life, you might find it interesting to learn that no one at work was aware of it. Why would she hide a passion that is such a big part of who she is? In reality, Carol felt uncomfortable telling her team about her painting hobby because she was afraid they would judge her as "unserious" or that they would view it as silly or frivolous. In short, she was heavily buying in to the professional norms described earlier.

When virtual work increased during the pandemic, Carol noticed that colleagues had artwork on their walls. Some even used their backgrounds to express themselves. She was intrigued. One day Carol decided to ask a team member about her background full of books. She quickly learned that this colleague loved to read and write and enjoyed feeling surrounded by books for inspiration. Carol walked away from the conversation feeling like she learned something new, interesting, and positive about her colleague. Noticing how positively she felt after learning this information, Carol considered, for the first time, sharing her artwork with her coworkers.

Deciding to take the plunge, she changed her Zoom background to one of her most recent paintings. Much to her surprise, when she entered her next meeting, the painting became an enthusiastic topic of conversation. Coworkers asked her how long she had been painting and what she liked to paint, and even inquired about her other hobbies. She felt really good about her decision to share her art. She felt even better when she realized later that her direct reports started sharing their own hobbies and passions with her. By sharing her authentic self, Carol had created a new way of deepening her relationships with her team members. In fact, she was surprised to realize how little she had known about her team before the Zoom meetings enabled people to share their passions. Carol quickly started becoming more of a Generator than an Extinguisher. She was able to build higher levels of trust on the team through her newfound authenticity and saw improvements in the team's overall morale.

Authenticity Can Be Contagious

In our research, we heard stories like Carol's time and time again. So many of our study participants were excited to tell us about how authentic leaders helped them open up and be real too. For example, Jelisa, a supply chain employee, shared:

> I wanted to have these vulnerable conversations with [my leader] because I did feel so safe with her. And I think a large part of that was because she did talk very openly about what was going on with her in her personal life. Her

daughter had an issue and she would talk a lot about that, and kind of how she was dealing with it.

Jelisa felt a real connection with her leader through the shared stories.

Monica, a data analyst at a large retailer, shared how her leader's authenticity helped her open up to him when dealing with her parent going through a challenging surgery:

> For better or worse, [my boss] is very forthcoming about his own life, and so, it made it pretty easy for me to be as forthcoming about what was going on with mine. So, in that sense, it was actually as easy as it can be to have that conversation, but it couldn't have been made any easier by him. . .if you don't know their family situation, if you don't hear when some of these things are happening, you're not really gonna be comfortable bringing them up when they happen to you. So I feel like his straightforwardness on a lot of those topics definitely set the tone for everyone else to be straightforward about what they're experiencing.

Monica talked about how grateful she was to be able to open up without any fear. She knew she could trust her leader with what she shared. This sharing also allowed her leader to support her effectively. He understood what she was facing and was able to adapt the work appropriately.

Both Jelisa and Monica felt safe and comfortable after their leaders shared themselves authentically at work. They went on to tell us how much they appreciated these leaders, how committed they were to working hard for them, and how proud they were to be on their teams. From a leader's perspective, Melanie and Carol grew closer to their team members, experienced improved well-being, and boosted team morale by firing their work selves and showing their employees a glimpse of who they really are. Take a moment to reflect on these stories. Have you experienced authenticity from a leader? What did you appreciate about it?

Take Action

Now it's time to take some action. What steps can you take to fire your work self and reengage with who you really are? We've included Worksheet 2.1 at the end of the chapter to help you reflect and identify some simple next steps to start your journey to being an authentic Generator.

As you begin your reflection, we have a few tips for you to consider:

- *Ask for help.* If you aren't sure if and when you are less authentic, ask a loved one to describe you. Then compare that description to a performance review or the feedback you've heard from your peers. Is there a disconnect? Does your best friend say you wear your heart on your sleeve but your boss says you are stoic and even-keeled? Look for the small differences between what people say about you in both realms.

- *Start small.* Melanie had a major personal insight to share with her team, but Carol started with sharing a fun hobby. Tiny steps in the right direction can have a major positive impact on your relationships and your authenticity at work.

- *Be patient.* Carol and Melanie saw returns on their authenticity, but it wasn't overnight. It took a few revelations for Carol's team to start to trust her, and that trust grew over time. Likely your team will take time to start showing their authentic selves. Keep working on your authenticity, and they will become comfortable enough to slowly follow your lead.

Now let's jump into the activity. You can use Worksheet 2.1 to document your thoughts or grab a notebook or computer—whatever works for you. Take fifteen to twenty minutes to work through the next steps and create a plan to become more authentic at work.

1. Write down three things that people at work don't know about you. These should be things that are somewhat important to you in your personal life. They can be positive and fun things, like Carol's love for painting. They could be more difficult things to share, like Melanie's loss. Regardless, these should be things about you that people in your personal life know. These might even be things that would surprise your loved ones if they learned that your coworkers didn't know about them.

2. Now that you have your list, arrange them in order from smallest to largest reveal. As mentioned, small reveals are always easier.

3. Start with your smallest reveal and think of three different ways to let your team know about this aspect of you. Maybe you could change your Zoom background, as Carol did. Or maybe you prefer to tell a story that incorporates this reveal at the next team happy hour. Or you might create an icebreaker activity at your next team meeting that allows people to share fun facts about themselves.

4. Repeat step 3 for the other reveals you listed. Get creative and consider sharing your reveal in multiple venues with different audiences.

5. Now that you have your plan for sharing your authentic self, act on it. Keep track of how people respond. Do you see any changes in your team's behavior? Notice what your team members say or share in response. Do you learn anything new about them? Do people act differently toward you right after or in the following days?

As you continue to make more reveals over the next few weeks, keep track of how people's responses and reactions to you change over time. As you slowly ease into sharing parts of yourself that you had kept hidden, you will find more opportunities to do so and get better at sharing your authenticity. Sharing will become more natural over time. Continue to keep track of how your relationships change and how your team dynamics change. And see how you can use what you learn about your team throughout this process to inform how you engage with them on a more personal level. (More on that in later chapters.)

While you may never fully fire your work self, becoming a Generator means bringing who you truly are and who you are at work closer together.

Key Takeaways

- Employees do not trust and do not want to work for inauthentic, "perfect" leaders. They are looking for leaders who show their true selves at work.

- Leaders fall prey to abiding by societal professional norms, thinking they are supposed to be "perfect."

- Authentic leaders are seen as trustworthy because employees believe they are more willing to be transparent and honest in all situations.

- Employees with authentic leaders are more productive, are more engaged, and have better well-being.

- Being authentic can be easier than you think. Start small with little details about yourself, like hobbies and interests.

Worksheet 2.1

Fire Your Work Self

Write down three things that people don't know about you at work.

Consider things about yourself that people in your personal life may be surprised to learn that you haven't shared at work.

1. _____
_____
_____
_____

2. _____
_____
_____
_____

3. _____
_____
_____
_____

Write down three ideas on how to share your authenticity for each of your revelations.

Reveal 1:
1. _____
_____
2. _____
_____
3. _____
_____

Reveal 2:
1. _____
_____
2. _____
_____
3. _____
_____

Reveal 3:
1. _____
_____
2. _____
_____
3. _____
_____

(Continued)

Keep Track of Responses

Do you see any changes in your team's behavior after sharing your revelations? Notice what your team members say or share in response. Did you learn anything new about them? Did people act differently toward you right after or in the following days?

_____
_____
_____
_____
_____
_____
_____
_____
_____
_____
_____
_____
_____
_____
_____
_____
_____
_____
_____
_____
_____
_____
_____
_____

Chapter 3

Embrace Your Struggle Statement

*So it's her sharing personal things about herself, that sort of
trust building. She's sharing. She's building that intimacy as
far as the personal relationship goes.*

—Julia, VP at a government agency, study participant

Struggling to succeed can seem embarrassing, especially to leaders. Acknowledging and sharing your hardships with the world
can be challenging—even more so when everyone is hiding their
struggles from others. When you aren't hearing about others' difficulties or worries in life, your challenges begin to feel like indicators
of your own weaknesses. The truth is, everyone struggles. But when
most people hide their struggles, grappling with tough tasks or situations can feel isolating or shameful. We've all been there, because
we are all human. It's also human to want to be accepted and viewed
positively by others. This need for acceptance fuels our desire to fit
in and to hide the parts of us that we think make us look weak or
different. But is concealing our true selves really the best we can do
for our own well-being or the well-being of our teams?

We start this chapter by asking you to let go of the version of
yourself that you project to the world and to connect to the real,
flawed version of yourself. Such letting go is no easy task. Reflecting
on their weaknesses naturally puts people into self-defense mode.
We are uncomfortable seeing ourselves in a realistic, accurate light.
But it's impossible to be vulnerable and open when we're focused

on protecting ourselves from discomfort. To avoid becoming overly self-protective, remember all the strengths that you bring to the table; those strengths are real, just like the challenges you face. Noticing what you are good at as you consider areas of struggle will help you to become more willing to recognize your weaknesses.

What's the point of seeing yourself in a more nuanced, and possibly more flawed, way? When you see yourself as you truly are—with all your strengths and weaknesses—you can become more comfortable with your complexities as a leader. We have talked about how much attention employees pay to leaders and how sharing your true self can help boost your authenticity at work. Now we shift our focus to actively sharing your work-related weaknesses with others. By showing your colleagues that it's okay to have weaknesses, you'll help them become more at ease with their own limitations. We've already talked about the importance of authenticity in your leadership. In this chapter, we take it a step further and talk more about the unique power of sharing your work-related struggles for creating happier and healthier work environments. But, for now, let go of your defensiveness and embrace the idea that you're human.

Time to Reflect

Now you're ready for a self-reflection that will shift you into the "struggle statement" mindset. Worksheet 3.1 at the end of the chapter can be used for this reflection.

1. Think of three to five things you are struggling with at work today. These can be anything, large or small. Perhaps you're having trouble finishing a task you find unenjoyable. Or maybe you're struggling interpersonally with a coworker and need to find a way to navigate conflict more effectively.

Whatever you're struggling with, call to mind a few of these challenges and reflect on them each for a minute or so.

2. Next think about three to five things you used to struggle with at work but have since overcome. In other words, think about a set of challenges that you used to face but you now can deal with effectively. Reflect on each of these challenges and take note of how you overcame each of them.

3. Write down these struggles in Worksheet 3.1, both present and past, and keep the worksheets handy for this chapter and your future action planning.

The worksheet of struggles will help you to formulate your struggle statement. Remembering how you overcame past challenges is useful for building resilience and motivation to work through new challenges. It can also help you communicate to others how you have found ways to work through struggles in the past.

Do you have your lists ready? Once you do, move on to the next section.

What Is a Struggle Statement?

In this chapter, we dig deeper into how to display vulnerability and authenticity, specifically regarding personal shortcomings and flaws. While the terms "vulnerability" and "authenticity" have similar meanings, they aren't exactly the same.

Vulnerability is the act of sharing or expressing information that is personal, emotional, and/or revelatory to others in a way that stands out from the norm. It can be hard to be vulnerable because others may react negatively or hurt your feelings. While we would never suggest that you become fully vulnerable to all people at work, or in your life, an appropriate amount of openness and vulnerability is important to bond people together.

Authenticity is achieved when you act in accordance with who you really are inside. Like vulnerability, we wouldn't suggest that people behave the exact same way at home as they do at work. As you learned in Chapter 2, professional norms and standards can be useful for setting the workplace apart from other, less formal life domains (e.g., spending time with friends or being at your child's soccer game). But you now know you should try to show the "real you" at work within professional bounds. Others take notice—in a bad way—when they think people at work are acting inauthentically.

Being vulnerable by sharing your work-related struggles requires a deeper dive into your own areas for improvement. It also entails recognizing when you might need help or fall short of expectations. Crafting a struggle statement is one way to become a more vulnerable and authentic leader. So, what is a struggle statement?

Struggle statements are statements that communicate hardships, setbacks, or weaknesses that make work more challenging for you. In Worksheet 3.1, you started working toward creating struggle statements by listing your challenges. Struggle statements are not the same as inspirational stories or tales about your admirable qualities in the face of hardships. Struggle statements show others that you have weaknesses at work too; they don't make others feel worse that they have been unable to overcome their challenges thus far.

If you're having trouble crafting your struggle statement, try completing one of these sentences:

- At work, I struggle with _____.

- As I complete my work tasks, I find it harder than most to _____.

- I haven't found a way to overcome _____ at work.

These are just a few possible ways to construct a struggle statement, but these phrases should help you to get started. Worksheet 3.1 has room for you to draft your statements. Draft as many as you can so you have multiple examples to share with your team.

> Start with a couple of easy struggle statements. It can be hard to be vulnerable about the big stuff right away. If you're struggling with writing statements about more difficult topics, consider writing progressively more vulnerable statements. For example, sharing that you have a hard time focusing in meetings that last longer than two hours may feel safer than sharing that you struggle with understanding budgets and have to go through refreshers each year. Both are perfectly reasonable struggles, but one might feel more common and the other might feel like you aren't good at your job. It may be much scarier to share the second struggle statement about having difficulty with budgets. It's okay to start small and get deeper as you build trust in your team. Eventually, that scarier struggle statement will help you get even further as a leader. You'll open the door to conversations that help people find ways to complement each other with their strengths. Maybe someone on your team is a budget wiz and they can step in and help. Imagine how much easier your job will become!

To model a good struggle statement, next we share an example based on a personal experience shared with us in a public forum at a diversity, equity, and inclusion workshop we attended awhile back. The story was so powerful that it has stuck with us for years. We hope it sticks with you too.

A Struggle Statement Story

Steve was a high-level banking leader who worked in a fast-paced, competitive company. In his view, if you weren't working 16-hour days and willing to drop everything at any time for your work, you weren't cut out for banking. As a leader, Steve ran his team in alignment with these views. He expected his team members to be available early mornings, evenings, and weekends. He wanted to see them working in the office so he knew they were following through on his vision for a productive team. On the surface, it looked like Steve's team was high performing. They were hitting their goals every quarter and often produced the best results compared to other banking teams.

But there was a hidden cost to Steve's team—turnover. In particular, he struggled to retain women. Although several women had worked on his team in the past, most didn't stay long. Steve thought that this was because banking was an industry only for employees who were willing to sacrifice everything for their careers. If women were leaving his team, it wasn't because of his leadership—it was because they weren't cut out for banking. Steve had a huge blind spot that prevented him from seeing the whole picture. He was married to his high school sweetheart, who was a stay-at-home parent, and they had four young daughters. Steve's wife took care of everything necessary to keep their home running effectively, while he took care of work outside of the house. In short, her household work and the time she spent on childcare supported his ability to be available to work long hours outside of the house, and at all times, day or night.

Then one day, tragically, Steve's wife was in a fatal car accident. Stricken with grief and disbelief, Steve became a single father of four overnight. He briefly took time away from work for bereavement and then returned to the office. On the first day Steve was to return, he began to realize some of the false assumptions he had made about the link between people's talents and skills and their willingness to give it all to work. Steve had always mandated a 7:00 am call for all team members. He thought that this early call helped everyone to get on the same page and set a strategy for the workday.

That time was convenient for him, and he assumed that dedicated employees would make that time work for them as well. On that day, however, one of Steve's daughters was really missing her mom. She was crying before leaving for school, saying she wanted to stay home. As Steve consoled her, the clock rolled right past 7:00 am and he missed the call.

In the days and weeks that followed, Steve had an epiphany. Maybe there was more than one way to be an outstanding banker. His talents and skills were no different than they had been, but his life circumstances had shifted. Perhaps the assumptions he had made about people—particularly women, who continue to bear more of the brunt of childcare and household duties even today—were wrong. Steve began to recognize that his own lack of flexibility and his inability to consider others' perspectives had kept him from realizing the potential of many great employees.

So, what did Steve do after his sudden realization? He shared his story with his team. He told them that he realized he struggled to see others eye to eye and that he wanted to do better to increase his ability to take others' perspective on the job. He said that he had a hard time overcoming his own assumptions about others and that he wanted to create an open environment where people could discuss their work-life struggles with him. And he made it clear that he wouldn't judge. Instead, he would use this information to help improve his leadership and the team environment. In addition, he continued to share his struggles in his new life openly. This openness helped his team understand it was okay to have struggles too. The team environment completely transformed from one of cutthroat competitiveness to one of compassion and collaboration.

Fast forward a few years—Steve's team was even more productive than before, and it had the highest number of women compared to all the other banking teams. Before Steve could share his struggle

43

with the team, he had to admit how his weaknesses were getting in his way at work. While Steve's example is extreme, we hope that his story helps you learn the same lesson in a much easier way. Once Steve recognized his struggle to see things from others' point of view, he shared this struggle with the team and everything changed for the better. After that, he continued to open up about his struggles and his team was willing to do the same.

Struggle Statements Matter

You may have resolved some of your struggles. Other struggles may be issues, tasks, or skills that you still need to work on and may never find a real solution for. For this reason, your struggle statement doesn't need to have a resolution at the end. You might share a struggle that has no real solution, and that's okay. For example, perhaps you're very introverted and you work in a job that requires you to interact with others frequently. You might share your ongoing struggles to muster the energy to interact with others for extended periods of time, telling your team that it's just something that takes more effort for you than for others—and that it likely always will. It's okay to share any resolution you may come to, if you feel that doing so might be helpful to the person you're sharing your struggle with. In this instance, it might be something like carving out some alone time to recharge after a long period of interpersonal interactions.

In our research, we found that participants mentioned how refreshing and useful it was for their leaders to share their struggles with them. For example, Daria, an HR analyst at a software company who was struggling with mental health challenges at work, shared that having an authentic relationship with her leader helped to create a more comfortable and welcoming work environment. She said:

I think just kind of leaning into [what's] authentic for the relationship between that manager and employee is really important. . .I think because there's this stigma around mental health, I think maintaining the [comfort] of the associate is always really important.

Similarly, Calla, an account manager at a health tech company, appreciated how her leader would discuss her struggles with team members. She shared: "She would talk about, in some capacity—her life, the struggles she was going through, how she's trying to combat [problems]." In all, we found that participants felt positively about leaders who were open and honest about their struggles, instead of hiding them or portraying an image of perfection. They didn't want their leaders to be superhuman. They wanted them to be real and humble enough to tell others about their flaws. They wanted leaders they could build real connections with, not people showing one thing on the surface but hiding something else deep down.

At first glance, employees' need for a vulnerable leader might seem counterintuitive. Doesn't everyone want a leader who has all the answers, who has all the skills needed to solve an issue or problem with ease, and who models how to do things the right way 100% of the time? As it turns out, no. People want leaders whom they can realistically aspire to be like and who are inspirational because they aren't perfect—but they try their best anyway.

Why a Struggle Statement?

Why do leaders' struggle statements have this somewhat counterintuitive positive effect at work? In our research, we found that when leaders share their struggles at work—either past or current—it leads to stronger and more positive relationships with their employees. These stronger relationships are built on trust. Similar to the effect firing your work self has in Chapter 2, you can build trust by being vulnerable.[1] This is because being vulnerable sends an important signal to others—that you trust them to know some of your weaknesses or areas of insecurity. Sharing your struggles is powerful because it shows others that you trust them enough to provide them with information that could put you at risk. Said differently, sharing is so powerful because you give coworkers the option of betraying your trust by exploiting these vulnerabilities. Leaders who share their vulnerabilities with others are essentially saying "I trust that you'll use this information to help me instead of to harm me." In the corporate world, where employees are often taught to be strategic, detached, and competitive, this kind of behavior stands out in a good way.

But doesn't sharing your weaknesses make people view you as less competent as a leader? We found that the opposite is true. Leaders are, for the most part, already assumed to have status and competence because of their positions. Generators are skilled at sharing their weaknesses and vulnerabilities without harming their competence. Although common wisdom may suggest that maintaining status and power hinges on some air of infallibility, our participants relayed that they much preferred leaders who were humble and willing to show others their flaws.

For example, Jordan, a manager in the defense industry, really appreciated hearing about his leader's struggles because it sent a message that his leader was "in it" with him, as opposed to feeling unbothered by their difficult work environment. Jordan also explained that these conversations aren't just gripe sessions or pity parties but rather a leader's willingness to recognize when struggles arise. He said:

> It's not misery loves company. But it's knowing that they're feeling frustrated about things going on in the job that I'm feeling frustrated about. And knowing that we're in it

together. Because a lot of times I feel some managers just always try to play it off as everything's going well, and "You just need to work hard and push through it." I don't think that that's a realistic perspective. And so during these one-on-ones with [my leader], he would tell me some of the struggles that he was dealing with professionally.

Because Jordan's leader was transparent about some of the challenges that he was facing at work, Jordan was more comfortable sharing what he was going through in his personal life as well. "On the personal side, we did talk about relationships and things. [He would ask] how was the girl [I was dating] at the time. We talked about that."

Some employees may have difficulty distinguishing between sharing struggles and having gripe sessions, which are unproductive. Although allowing space for people to vent frustrations and share emotional reactions is important, encouraging productive discussions about struggles is more valuable and does not breed unnecessary negativity in the team.

Let's say you have a colleague who struggles with remembering decisions that are made. They move quickly from meeting to meeting and often forget where things landed. Frustrating, right? An employee may want to complain about this situation every time it happens. Venting actually can be helpful, but we suggest that you encourage the employee not to dwell on the frustrating situation. Instead, redirect the conversation to possible solutions to mitigate the problem. Or coach employees on how to provide feedback to the colleague. Alternatively, you can share a

(Continued)

Embrace Your Struggle Statement

(Continued)

struggle statement of your own about when you dealt with a difficult colleague in the past and how you handled it.

If, even with redirection, an employee continues to complain and vent about the stakeholder, consider providing that employee with direct feedback. Thank them for sharing their challenges and struggles. Then explain that dwelling on the negative can breed more negativity instead of promoting positive solutions. Unfortunately, we all deal with frustrations at work that cannot be changed easily. However, our mindset in handling those situations is critical.

Jordan's example highlights how, when leaders show vulnerability and employees view it as authentic, employees feel empowered to be themselves. When leaders share that they aren't perfect or have areas to work on, employees feel that they can also express themselves more freely.[2] Importantly, they also trust leaders more not to exploit their weaknesses, since leaders trusted them with the same responsibility.

Why is leader vulnerability important for the bottom line? In addition to creating a team culture that is more supportive and connected, which we discuss in depth in Chapter 4, leader vulnerability is also shown to be better for team performance. Beyond building stronger, more trusting relationships with employees, leaders can drive important work outcomes when they are open to sharing their weaknesses. In fact, research on leader humility shows that employees are more satisfied with leaders who are willing to recognize their own limitations.[3] Humble leaders also tend to have higher-performing teams.[4] Thus, embracing your struggle statement can really help your team connect to the real you while also boosting team attitudes and effectiveness.

Sharing Leads to More Sharing

One of the key outcomes associated with leader vulnerability and authenticity is that it encourages employees to act in the same way. We found that, as Generators shared their struggle statements, employees began to share their own. Remember Melanie from Chapter 2 who lost her sibling? Over time, her team was transformed from one that was buttoned up and less authentic, to being one that was open, honest, and more real. Indeed, research shows that vulnerability is contagious.[5] Melanie's story exemplifies this well. These changes in her team also provoked Melanie to share a struggle statement. Specifically, she recounted how challenging it was to manage her work and life during the pandemic—a real hurdle that many people faced during the lockdown and beyond. She told us:

> I'm gonna be open and honest that it was a struggle for me, a huge struggle for me at the start of COVID when I was working and kids were home. I had a [baby and a toddler], and trying to balance parenting with working, and having zero time for me, and just really being exhausted— and having mommy guilt and worker guilt and—all of that was a real, big struggle. And so I was very vocal with my team at that time about those struggles that I went through and trying to figure out a way to regain some control over my life where I felt like I had completely lost all control. And so I shared with them. . .my journey and seeking help for that and working through anxiety and getting medications to help me through that as well so that I could be present and healthy and whole.

The vulnerability that Melanie showed helped her team members to become more willing to share their own struggles. Ultimately, she created an environment where employees were more open and honest about their shortcomings. This was useful to Melanie, as the leader, because she now understood more about what her team was grappling with as they approached their work. Melanie shared the impact that her vulnerability had on her team, recounting:

> And it opened the door for others to start sharing their mental health struggles, and they would do so in our one-on-ones. Which was really refreshing—to hear that it mattered to them and that they were curious. And I would even be vocal about some of the resources that I would get through my therapy and my experience. And I had many requests for, you know, the details, or "Can you share any handouts that you would get?"

Melanie's story is a testament to the power of leaders sharing a struggle statement. She was able to gain new insights about her team that she never would have uncovered if she hadn't modeled being open about weaknesses. And she was better able to help her team with what they were struggling with because they were more willing to share their challenges with her, and each other. It's important to remember that your team is constantly working through challenges, whether you know it or not. In this case, ignorance isn't bliss. If you aren't aware of the challenges your team members face, you can't help them to work through, or around, them. Making it safe to share struggles is key to understanding the realities your team is facing on a day-to-day basis. Nothing about the challenges that Melanie's team members were facing changed, but now everyone was aware of what others were going through. In this way, unaddressed struggles of team members could be better supported, alleviated, or even eliminated.

Share Your Struggle Statement

Now that you've read about the power of sharing a struggle statement, it's time for you to think about sharing yours. Look back at the lists you created at the start of the chapter and in Worksheet 3.1. Choose one of the struggles that you listed there. If you found this chapter particularly motivating, you may be tempted to share all the struggles on your list. However, as a Generator, it's important not to share all your struggles in one sitting. Sharing too many weaknesses at once can overwhelm employees or make you seem like an oversharer. Choose one for now. As you're selecting your struggle, keep in mind that it's perfectly okay to choose the one that's easiest for you to share. You're just starting out on this journey, and it's not necessary to reveal something that is truly difficult to discuss. Especially if this is the first time you're disclosing a struggle to others, we give you permission to start small and work your way up.

Once you have selected your struggle, consider whether there is anything you'd like to update now that you've heard other statements and stories. Take a moment to tweak anything that needs adjusting. Do you need to get clearer on what the weakness you're disclosing actually is? Do you have a specific example of a time when your struggle got in your way at work? Are you able to communicate how you're coping with that weakness? Or is your statement less "fixable" and more about an ongoing battle you'll have to grapple with in the long term? Once you finalize your statement, you can move on to thinking about how to share it with others on your team.

> Being vulnerable sends an important signal to others—that you trust them to know some of your weaknesses or areas of insecurity. Sharing your struggles is powerful because it shows others that you trust them enough to provide them with information that could put you at risk.

It's important to consider how to integrate your struggle statements into interactions with your team. First, you might want to share your struggle statement with someone who seems like they might struggle with something similar. For example, Jason, an executive at a medical device company, credits his leader, Amelia, for helping him to avoid burnout during a very stressful time. During a high-pressure project, Amelia noticed that Jason and his colleagues were working long hours and showing signs of stress. In a team meeting, Amelia told the team her personal experience with burnout early in her career. After she shared her struggle statement, the team could recognize that they were struggling with the same issues. Importantly, this sharing also brought the team together to prioritize work-life balance more consciously. Jason said that Amelia's story made the team feel more comfortable sharing their challenges openly. Team members were enabled to support each other more fully, because the issues they were facing were out in the open, instead of being buried or ignored.

You can also share a struggle statement unprompted, simply because you are genuinely feeling challenged by something in your work environment. In such a case, bring up the struggle statement whenever it's relevant. For example, you might bring it up when you're discussing a project you're struggling with, or when you're talking about how to execute on a plan that you know you're going to have a harder time with than most. We found that most leaders who share their struggle statements unprompted did so during a team meeting or all-hands call, to give their struggle statement the greatest amount of visibility and impact. Such meetings might be natural times to discuss your struggle because specific projects and plans for action are discussed in team meetings. Not ready to make your statement quite so visible? Sharing in a smaller group environment, or one on one, is fine. The main takeaway here is that you don't have to know that someone else is sharing a similar struggle to make it okay for you to share yours. Simply having a struggle is reason enough to share it.

Finally, you might share a struggle statement when you know your team is about to encounter challenges to their progress, or if they are already finding it difficult to achieve their goals. In this instance, you might discuss a time in your career when you failed to achieve results or when you had to find creative ways to get around your shortcomings to progress. When people are actively struggling to be successful, sometimes it helps to hear that others have been there too. It's hard to be motivated by folks who seem to have never faced a similar challenge. Instead, the opposite may happen. As employees are toiling to meet goals, they may find others who seemingly lack these struggles as too dissimilar to pay attention to. By showing your employees that you recognize, understand, and have shared their struggles, you help them to understand that they too will survive and move on eventually.

Whenever you decide to share your struggles, you will make a positive impact by doing so. It's hard to share your struggles with the world. But we believe it's worth it, and our research shows the same. Push yourself out of your comfort zone and show others that it's okay to have flaws. We all have them. Being authentic with others about your struggles knits people together, instead of keeping them siloed, facing undisclosed challenges on their own. Even more, teams that are more interconnected, honest, and trusting of one another perform better too. The next time you hesitate to show your weaknesses with your team, remember that sharing things you struggle with could be the very thing that helps your team to do its best.

Key Takeaways

- Struggle statements are simply challenges or difficulties you face at work—both past and present.

- Being open with your employees about your struggles can build trust and help them open up to you. Research consistently shows that employees do not want infallible leaders.

- Teams that are open about their struggles, in a safe and judgment-free environment, are more productive and higher performing.

- Start small as you begin to share your struggle statements and build up to the harder things over time, as you continue to build trusting relationships with your employees.

Worksheet 3.1

Embrace Your Struggle Statement

Let's start with a reflection.

List three things that you are struggling with at work today. These can be big or small.

1. _____
   _____
   _____
   _____
   _____

2. _____
   _____
   _____
   _____
   _____

3. _____
   _____
   _____
   _____
   _____

List three things you used to struggle with but have overcome. Note how you overcame these struggles.

1. _____
   _____
   _____
   _____
   _____
   _____

2. _____
   _____
   _____
   _____

3. _____
   _____
   _____
   _____

(Continued)

Embrace Your Struggle Statement

Draft Your Struggle Statements

Take the struggles you listed above and create six struggle statements. The first three should focus on what you are still struggling with today. The last three should be struggle statements from the past. These six statements should help you relate to others who are struggling.

Try these as starting points:

1) "I struggle with _____."
2) "I find it harder than most to _____."
3) "I haven't found a way to overcome _____."
4) "I used to have a hard time with _____."
5) "Early in my career, I couldn't figure out how to _____."

_____
_____
_____
_____
_____
_____
_____
_____
_____
_____
_____
_____
_____
_____
_____
_____
_____
_____
_____

Part II

It's the Tone, Not the Time

Now that we have discussed the importance of being open and vulnerable with your team about your own joys, worries, skills, and shortcomings, we are going to turn toward cultivating a positive team culture. In this part, we reveal the second core component of becoming a Generator—recognizing that setting the right tone is more important than putting in the most time. Contrary to most working conventions, we show that Generators don't outwork their counterparts. Rather, they excel at leading their team because of *how* they lead, not because of how much time they spend on the job. We highlight the two key sets of behaviors that comprise this pillar of Generator leadership—setting the right tone and swiftly becoming a confidant.

Chapter 4

Set the Right Tone

We're all working together in a more cohesive way. And I think that the tone of that is set a lot by. . .leadership, in part, because they make the hiring decisions, right? But also because the way that people present work in those broader team meetings, the way that those incentives are handed out—it can create either a competitive or a collaborative [environment]. And so there is an element of the day-to-day running of things that can support that culture or. . .not.

— Monica, data analyst, study participant

What is the current tone of your team? Is that the right tone, or could it be improved? It can be hard to know for sure. There are so many different types of team cultures—from compassionate and caring, to independent and hands-off, to cutthroat and competitive. Plus, you've probably met people who claim that each of these types of cultures produces results. What is the *best* tone to set for a team? Luckily, our research, and the research of many other organizational scholars, has an answer for you. The science-backed answer is simple: People want to work in an environment where they feel happy and fulfilled as whole people. The right tone and culture breeds happiness in employees.

So, what's the secret to creating the right tone? We found that Generators create a team culture that allows employees to break free of traditional definitions of what it means to be an "ideal" employee and instead to focus on being an exemplary team member who builds others up and helps them out. We also learned that Generators focus not only on setting the right tone for their team but also on rewarding team members who do the same thing. By rewarding the behaviors they want to see more of, Generators see these behaviors catch on throughout the team. In turn, their team becomes more self-sufficient, helping Generators spend less time managing. Their teams do the right thing when no one is looking, help each other solve problems, and have less interpersonal conflict and misunderstandings.

This chapter gives you the key insights and tools for you to create the right tone for your team as you embark on your journey to become a Generator. We argue that leaders can engage in two key sets of behaviors to make sure that the tone of their team encourages feelings of fulfillment and happiness:

1. Modeling a positive work-life balance
2. Recognizing the power of positivity and gratitude in creating a self-sustaining, happy work environment

This chapter covers both behaviors in detail.

Role Modeling a Positive Work-Life Balance

Before we dive into the topic of role modeling, let's do a quick reflection. We find that this reflection helps senior leaders focus on the *impact* of their behaviors.

> *Imagine yourself working on a typical workday. You are doing what you normally do to get your work done and ensure your team's success. Now imagine your team members are following you around with clipboards taking notes*

on your actions and behaviors. Imagine them writing down every tiny detail of your day. What time did they write down that you started working? Did you answer emails on your phone as soon as your eyes popped open in the morning? Imagine them noting how many breaks you took and how many meals you ate in front of your computer. Did they see you cancel any personal plans? Or shorten your dinnertime with your family? Did they witness you disconnecting at the end of the day or answering more emails? Now imagine that every team member uses these notes and replicates your actions and behaviors each and every day.

Our culture teaches us that the best leaders are constantly busy, always on, and work endlessly to make sure that their company is successful. They lean in and do everything they can to exceed goals and expectations set for their teams. They shoulder the extra burden when it's all hands on deck. Leaders who behave this way are focused on fulfilling the image of an ideal worker. As discussed in Chapter 2, we've been taught as a society that ideal workers constantly put work first over everything else, sacrificing their personal lives whenever work beckons. But this mentality is very shortsighted, and we take issue with it. This view fails to account for the downsides of the so-called ideal—burnout, disengagement, and everything we've already highlighted that can stem from overwork.

Ideal worker norms are pervasive in our working lives in ways we don't even notice. Stemming from traditional work arrangements, in which it was much more common for men to focus solely on working outside of the home and for women to focus solely on working inside of the home, ideal worker norms tell us that work

(Continued)

61

Set the Right Tone

(Continued)

should be the most important—or even the only—responsibility in any employee's life. Even as more women have entered the workforce, this outdated norm continues to persist: that work should be top priority over anything else.

Recognizing the ways in which ideal worker norms seep into our lives and into our expectations of others can be hard. When push comes to shove, do you think that work should always take priority over life? Do you react negatively to stories about people who turned down work opportunities to pursue life opportunities?

Understanding how ideal worker norms are embedded in the way you think and work can provide good insights as you try to shift away from these norms over time.

Trying to live up to this ideal worker image is harmful for any employee, but it's particularly detrimental for leaders. Consider your earlier reflection. What do you think would happen if your team members mimicked your every move? Maybe you are already on the right track and following your lead would result in team members setting clear boundaries and taking more time for themselves. But we venture to guess that you probably have some bad habits you don't want team members to emulate. Would they be following you on a quest to be an ideal worker? What would happen if they spent their whole day in back-to-back meetings like you, making up the working time at night or early in the morning, sacrificing their time to disconnect and recover from work? They would be setting themselves up for burnout and poor performance—just like you are. No one wants to face burnout or feel like they aren't doing well at work. So, are you setting a good example?

When you become a leader, you can't expect people to do as you say and not as you do. People pay attention to and replicate your actions. They look to you to understand how to get ahead. Your employees want to know what it takes. Setting a bad example solidifies bad behavior for future leaders. What do Generators do instead?

Generators Practice What They Preach

Generators recognize that they do not need to achieve the ideal worker image. Instead, they know that a leader's role is all about *impact*. Generators understand that when employees closely monitor their actions, they reverberate more intensely through the team than they did when they were an individual contributor. They consider how those behaviors impact their team's long-term success. As a result, these leaders choose to act differently. Instead of focusing on the amount of time that they are working, Generators think about the example they want to set.

Nia, an HR employee at a small software company, shared with us that her leader was effective at disconnecting from email. That led the team to do the same. She said:

> I think she sets the tone in that—well, holiday weekends are a really great [example]. She'll send a group text message to everybody, but it's not technically work-related—it's just a text message—at 3:00 pm and be like, "I'm really grateful to have you on my team, but you all need to clock out and stop working. I don't want you to look at email over this weekend. Take the time and enjoy the time off. Spend time with your family and do things that feed you." She's not going to answer emails over a holiday weekend, or over regular weekends, even. She's very, "When I'm done for the day, I'm

done for the day, and you should be, too." She expects us to be, I don't know if the word is "mature enough" to know when to stop, but [there's] just that expectation.

Nia's leader is a great example of a Generator who not only communicates her expectations but lives up to them. She encourages her team to disconnect and does so herself, in a very visible way, setting the tone for the rest of the team to follow.

Another study participant, Jake, a high-performing manager for a major consulting firm, shared that he benefited from taking time on the weekend and on his days off to hike and get out into nature. He had a high-pressure, client-facing job, and the time away from work was critical for his mental wellness. Under his prior leader, Jake felt like he was never able to fully get lost in nature. He was expected to be on call in case anything came up while he was out of the office. As a result, Jake was never fully able to disconnect. He saw things improve when his leader changed. His new leader, Carlos, told the team that he would respect their work-life boundaries and that he expected the team to extend him the same courtesy. Carlos modeled these behaviors by fully disconnecting when engaging in his own hobbies and family events. His behavior promoted the idea that nothing is so urgent that it requires an immediate response and that having a life outside of work is important. The team quickly adapted and learned not to ping each other during their downtime. Jake was finally able to fully get lost in nature on his hikes and benefited greatly from his ability to truly disconnect.

Similarly, Rashida, a senior leader at a small consulting firm, recalled how she felt when her leader broke with a culture of overwork to protect his own and his employees' time:

We received survey results about increased stress or burnout or seeing other leaders who were saying "No, you don't have to put in these crazy hours to be successful. But ignore the fact that I'm online at 3:00 am." My manager actually had individual and team discussions with our team, saying "I don't support this." And he was actually pretty good about protecting his weekends and not going into the evenings or the mornings sending requests or actions at crazy hours. There are those strange moments in the world. . .where maybe there is a weekend where you're working through, because there is a tight deadline. You can do that, but it's the exception rather than the rule. So [that manager] both did the talk and he did the walk, which was very nice.

Rashida made it abundantly clear that employees notice when leaders don't follow the expectations or advice they give their teams. She greatly appreciated working with a leader who was consistent in what he said and did. His behavior helped clarify what the real expectations were.

Nia, Jake, and Rashida all shared examples of times that their leaders showed employees that they not only could, but they should, take time away from their work to focus on their lives. The leaders not only communicated their expectations to the team but also disconnected themselves. These Generators participated in activities they enjoyed, didn't respond to people while they were out of the office, and encouraged their teams to follow suit. These leaders recognized and harnessed the power of their own example and used it to create a team culture that helped everyone to thrive—including themselves.

Leaders' Actions Impact Culture

Ultimately, the main takeaway from our findings is that leaders' actions matter more for determining team culture than leaders often recognize. You can't tell employees to do one thing and then you do another. In other words, as the adage says, actions speak louder than words. In our research, Generators showed their employees that having a life is okay, that being away from work is a natural and important part of life, and that even leaders need to take time for themselves. Instead of hiding or being embarrassed by their own downtime, they shared it with others and encouraged their team to do the same.

Remember Asher, the leader at a tech startup who was coping with a cancer diagnosis, from Chapter 1? He had so many great examples and stories to share about the Generators in his workplace. Asher shared a formal practice that his leaders used to instill a team culture where life was just as important as work. His leaders focused on moments of joy that not only meant something to employees but allowed them to share the fullness of their lives with others on their team:

> We are kind of expected to go out and have fun and then come back and tell the company about it—what we did over the weekend that was really awesome and what we enjoyed. Every time we have a company all-hands meeting, we have a little part of the meeting where we all talk about "I went to this great concert this weekend. It was awesome and this is why it was great," or "We went to this great restaurant in town and it's so great you guys should try it." And that's just part of our work time. And we have an entire channel on Slack that's [just for sharing] joy. And it's just about talking about this great time that we had over the weekend or on our vacation—and I say [it's] expected but it's more like we're encouraged to pick the time to do that, which I think is really special in an American work culture where sometimes those things are thought of as

"That's a waste of your work time. You're wasting the company's time on conversations that don't deal specifically with work."

Asher raved about the culture these practices created. His leaders not only modeled making time for their personal lives but made sure it was talked about and applauded. Publicly sharing and celebrating employees' lives outside of work helps embed these expectations into the team culture and mindset. Over time, there's no question as to whether employees are allowed to take time to disconnect from work. They just do it—and new team members follow suit.

Modeling work-life balance isn't just about setting the tone for your team to have long, happy, and productive work lives; it's also about setting the wheels in motion for a self-sustaining culture that does the same. When these avenues to discuss work and life exist in a workplace, and when employees are encouraged to share their joys virtually and in person, employees start encouraging each other to lead full and happy lives. In such cases, the leader's impact scales more rapidly. Asher's leaders are now able to rely on the whole team to continually reinforce the culture they'd like to see. Building this type of self-sustaining culture helps maximize the leader's impact. Generators focus on modeling work-life balance so that they can continue shaping the culture of their team, even when they aren't around.

In contrast, one of our participants shared an example of an Extinguisher who set the wrong tone—one of overwork and a lack of balance. Ella, a consultant at a top global firm, recounted:

> I think that the people above me work a lot and I'm sure that does sneak into my brain even though it's not like a mandate that they make for me. But they work late. And the people who work right below them—their staff that

are trying to be the next level as that boss—they are working a lot of hours. So I guess that is implying at this level we are expected to work a lot of hours.

Ella made our point for us. Employees watch what their leaders do and use it as information about what their leaders' expectations are, especially when it comes to growth and promotion. As a leader, your actions are not just things you do; they set expectations for others to follow. Being conscious about what expectations you're setting, and focusing on healthy work-life balance as a goal, is critical for your journey to becoming a Generator and not an Extinguisher.

> Modeling work-life balance isn't just about setting the tone for your team members to have long, happy, and productive work lives; it's also about setting the wheels in motion for a self-sustaining culture that ultimately does the work for you.

Creating a Positive Work Environment

Setting the right tone includes more than creating the right expectations for how work and life balance together. Generators also ensure that their teams are characterized by positivity, gratitude, and a shared willingness to help or support a teammate when they need it. Creating this type of team environment may seem like a big effort, but, surprisingly, it's quite simple. As we'll discuss further, positivity leads to more positivity. Generators know this. But, instead of thinking of themselves as a hub from which all positivity, gratitude, and help must originate, Generators build the capacity for their teams to sustain a happy and productive team culture independently.

Improving a team's capacity to build and maintain the right team tone is much more time efficient than thinking you should be the only person driving it. When leaders view themselves as the main source of positivity on their team, driving the right tone takes a lot of time and effort. Such leaders then have to be the ones to bring people together, provide positive encouragement and feedback, thank them for their contributions, and help when they have a personal or professional struggle. Doing this for every individual team member can be overwhelming, and often it's impossible. In fact, one of the first reactions we hear from leaders when talking about creating a positive team environment is "I don't have the time!" We've repeatedly heard that leaders don't have time for constant one-on-ones each week. They don't have time to tell their employees what they are thankful for every few days. They don't have time to bring the team together to socialize and have fun. They don't have time to answer every question and help with every challenge their team members face. These leaders are completely right. They probably don't have the time to do all these things, day in and day out.

Yes, Generators do all these things sometimes—but not *all the time*. They recognize the power of contagious positivity and use it to create a culture where team members support each other. Generators aren't the only ones thanking employees for their contributions. They aren't planning social time for the team solo. And they aren't the lone problem solver stepping in and helping when someone has a question or needs support. In the cultures Generators create, employees do the right thing, even when leaders aren't watching.

Research Supports Contagious Positivity

Research shows that positive emotions are contagious.[1] When you see others being and feeling positive, you also experience more positivity. Over time, when you and others show positive emotions at work, those emotions start to become part of the culture. Classic research in this area shows that we mimic others' emotions as a way to bond with them. As people mimic one another's positivity on the team, showing encouragement and spreading good vibes becomes the norm. When teams have norms of positivity, they are more likely to see the good in their own situations and spread positive emotions to others, even in the face of challenges.[2] This is called *broad-minded coping*. Broad-minded coping is the idea that, when life doesn't go the way that you wanted, your team's positivity can help you see the bigger picture, show you that there may be silver linings to challenges you face, and remind you that better times are likely around the corner. Ultimately, broad-minded coping helps keep the tone of a team positive through difficult times.

As positive emotions are built into a team's culture over time, the team's tone can help defend against negative emotion spirals. Unfortunately, negative emotions are also contagious—sometimes even more contagious than positive ones.[3] However, a team tone that is positive and full of upbeat emotions can buffer negative emotion spirals employees may experience in stressful times. Positive emotions help shift employees away from focusing on the stress. They broaden employees' perspectives to recognize more positive elements of the situation they are facing. Positive emotions help employees stay focused on the present, even when the future may seem challenging. Setting the tone for positivity on the team is not only important for making teams happy, but it can also help them manage through tougher times.

Positive emotions can help to broaden your team's appreciation for the good people and occurrences in their work environments. Negative emotions, in contrast, narrow your team's focus onto stressors and crowd out attention toward more positive elements of their working lives.

Think about receiving an extremely stressful email or phone call. When you receive distressing information, your mind becomes locked in on that information and doesn't make room for much else. If someone brought you a cup of coffee while you were responding to that stressful email or phone call, you might not even notice the gesture.

This narrowed attention is helpful, at times, because more resources are required to cope with stressful situations than positive or neutral ones. But these defaults can get in the way when stressors don't require that much attention or when other, more positive aspects of work or others' behaviors are being missed. Consistently spreading positivity can help to counter these negative emotion spirals.

We found similar patterns in our own research, where we saw that positivity spreads from Generators to their teams. We've mentioned Kassie before—a senior leader at a boutique consulting firm. She shared how her leader set a lighthearted and positive tone in meetings, which spread throughout the team to create a broader culture of positivity. She recounted:

We generally have a pretty light tone to our meetings. Nobody is particularly serious at our internal meetings. And I think we also have really strong norms for helping each other and being responsive to each other. Because that's one of the things that struck me when I first joined the organization. I would send an email needing a piece of information, and the person would get back to me with it immediately. Or if they did that to me and I responded, they would be like "Thank you so much. This is helpful." And when I was in [my prior place of work], that just didn't happen. It was kind of like pulling teeth to get the information that you needed. [Supervisors] were often unresponsive. Certainly, nobody was thanking me for very much.

Kassie went on to describe how team members grew so accustomed to, and fond of, these norms that they even helped new hires curb behaviors that would contradict them. She continued:

Such strong norms for information sharing and responsiveness and helping your fellow coworkers is a great thing. So, I think that's another thing that I find to be unique about our culture, and I think it also really helps to discourage any sort of competitiveness. There was actually an incident where someone from another company joined. And it kind of seemed like she was making an attempt to go after a client that I was going to pursue. And she was actually counseled by her leadership on "You can't steal this work from Kassie's team. If you want to work with Kassie's team, that is fine. But you can't just go steal it."

Kassie's firm was a great example of keeping a positive culture and maintaining it by ensuring the right norms were upheld continuously. In this way, positive team norms become self-fulfilling. When positivity, encouragement, and support become just the way things are done, the team culture requires far less of the leader's time to sustain. Instead, the whole team maintains the culture, by continuously reinforcing it through their own actions and behaviors.

Gratitude Is Also Contagious

Gratitude is a specific type of positive emotion. When you express gratitude, you are sharing and feeling a sense of thankfulness to someone else for their actions or efforts. Maybe you've noticed the popularity of starting a personal, daily gratitude practice, using a gratitude journal. Although focusing on gratitude seems like a nice idea, a lot of research supports the importance of gratitude in many aspects of life. And, relevant for our purposes, it's important in the workplace as well. Creating a culture of reciprocity and gratitude has many benefits for teams. When you thank someone for their efforts, they feel more connected and thankful to you in return.[4] Thus, employees who receive gratitude are more likely to give gratitude to others. This is called a *gratitude spiral*. Spirals of gratitude occur when people continue to pay forward to others the thanks they receive. When employees feel seen and recognized by others, they pass on the gratitude to their colleagues, helping build a positive work environment.

Setting the tone for gratitude does take an initial investment of time. Leaders have to spend time thanking their teams in a way that is consistent enough to catch on. How do you create that consistency? Just like any other habit, it takes some time, reminding, and practice.

A Generator we both admire used a physical reminder to practice gratitude. He put three coins in his pocket each day and set a goal to move each coin to a different pocket whenever he showed gratitude to others at work. He did this for months until it became a habit. Once he got into the habit of showing gratitude three times a day, he no longer needed the coins. And, by this point, his team had started to mimic his behaviors. They were sharing gratitude just as frequently. You can do this exercise yourself with any object or even sticky notes on your laptop that you move from one side to the other. However you can best remind yourself, go for it; your gratitude practice will start paying off, maximizing your ability to impact your team's overall culture.

Role Modeling Helping Leads to More Helping

Just as gratitude begets gratitude, it also provokes employees to pay forward the actions they are grateful for. In this way, Generators do a great job of building a team that not only spreads positivity and thankfulness but also creates self-sustaining cycles of reciprocal helping and support between team members. Again, this helping cycle all starts with modeling these behaviors as a leader.

Research shows that when employees witness someone else helping a team member, they themselves are inspired to help someone.[5] In the academic literature, we call this behavior *prosocial conformity*. It's the idea that people help others more when they see other people do it. In one study, Dr. Erik Nook and his colleagues conducted a set of experiments that show prosocial conformity in action.[6] Study participants were asked to donate to a charity. Before they decided how much, they learned what others donated. If they heard about a generous donation, they were much more likely to be generous in their donation than if they heard about a small donation. Not only that, after hearing about an anonymous peer giving a larger donation, they were also more likely to directly help someone in need who was described as being in a situation unrelated to their prior donation. Just knowing that someone else was helpful is enough for others to "catch" helpful behaviors.

Generators set the tone of helping by helping others first. Importantly, they don't hide their helpfulness from view. Instead, they visibly help team members, stepping in to do tasks that other leaders are unlikely to do. This behavior sets the expectation of helping and motivates team members to step up and help each other too. As you can imagine, helping behavior is an important pillar of any healthy, thriving team.

As we dive into topics like flexibility in later chapters, you will see how critical it is for team members to come together in support of others. As a leader, you cannot carry the burden of helping everyone, all the time, by yourself. Thus, setting the tone for helping in your team's culture is a major early step in your journey to becoming a Generator.

A Word of Caution

Creating a positive team culture can help you and your team be happier and healthier in your work lives. However, it is important to not let this tone bleed into a culture of *toxic positivity*. As with anything, there's a balance. Suppressing negative or bad emotions is not the answer to a positive work culture. It's important to recognize the positive in tough situations and highlight joy in a challenging journey, but it's also important to work through negative emotions productively. A fake positive culture will be obvious and won't feel authentic.

Mia, a recruiter at a recruiting firm, talked about how recognizing and honoring a range of emotions helped her team to process negative emotions together. She felt like it helped her team deal with difficult emotions more productively and to put their struggles into a broader perspective. Mia shared:

> Every leadership meeting started with every person [going] around the room and say[ing] one word that described how [they] were feeling. And it was really insightful and it allowed people to say how they were feeling and not have to feel guilty. And lots of people cried and felt overworked and stressed. But it gave them an outlet. And it was a big team. There were probably 25 of us. So it wasn't so we could sit and talk about every person's emotions. But it was a great opportunity—you could go to someone and say "How can I help you? What can I do?" And so I've taken that with me to my next jobs. And at [my current employer], we try to start our weekly meetings with a gut

check. "How does everybody feel? What's going on?" And sometimes someone will say "I saw your email at 10:00 pm last night. Are you taking care of yourself?"

In Mia's example, the expression of negative emotions helped others know where support was needed. While being overly negative can create major problems, sharing negative emotions, thoughts, or challenges in a generally positive team culture helps determine what to fix. As you learned in Chapter 3, struggle statements are important. Generators create a balanced, positive, grateful, and helpful team culture that can handle negative emotions, challenges, and problems as they arise. They don't shy away from those challenges, but they don't dwell on them either.

Improve Your Own Habits

It can be hard to deprogram yourself as a leader who focuses on the time you put in versus the tone that you set. But, with practice, you can create a culture that makes it easier for your employees to help each other to be happy and healthy. This culture will save you time in the long run and help you to achieve your results the right way. We encourage you to start to take actions today to shift the culture. Use Worksheet 4.1 at the end of the chapter to define your first steps to setting the right tone.

In the worksheet, start by identifying the good habits you already have, where you may need improvement, and which habits you'd like to add.

- Start by considering what you are already doing well. What examples are you setting that you hope catch on? For example, maybe you already disconnect from email after hours. Great! Make a note of that habit as something you want to continue and highlight for others to follow your example.

- Next, think about where you may need to fix your habits. Are you eating your lunch during meetings with your team? Are they beginning to do the same? Make note of when the example you are setting isn't ideal or healthy.

- Finally, think about what habits you may want to add. Maybe you aren't expressing gratitude consistently with your team. Make note that you want to begin thanking your team members frequently throughout the week.

Once you've identified what example you want to set, start thinking about how to do that. How can you make sure people see those good habits? What can you do to change the bad ones? And how will you build those new habits? Write down concrete steps you can take over the next several weeks to start setting the right tone for your team.

Key Takeaways

- Modeling work-life balance and prioritizing your personal life helps set an example and expectation for team members to follow.

- Positive emotions and gratitude are contagious. If you share positive emotions and gratitude with your employees, they will start to spread that same positivity.

- Employees are inspired to help others if they see team members helping each other.

- Creating a culture of work-life balance, positivity, gratitude, and helping is self-sustaining, because employees "catch" the right behaviors. This type of team culture saves you time in the long term.

Worksheet 4.1

Set the Right Tone

Take a moment to reflect on the example you are currently setting. What are you doing well? What can you do better? What should you be doing that you aren't doing already?

Think about things you are doing to set an example for a healthy work-life balance and how you are creating positivity and gratitude on the team. Make notes below.

Habits I want to continue

Habits I need to change

Habits I want to add

Set the Right Tone

Review your list of habits and create concrete steps to start showcasing, changing, or adding these habits.

Steps to make my good habits more visible:

1. _____
   _____

2. _____
   _____

3. _____
   _____

Steps to change my bad habits:

1. _____
   _____

2. _____
   _____

3. _____
   _____

Steps to start my new habits:

1. _____
   _____

2. _____
   _____

3. _____
   _____

Chapter 5

Swiftly Become a Confidant

[My leader] was very good about talking through how I felt or asking questions. [He would talk to me] with a spirit of inquiry and then reflect back and mirror back [what I said]. [He was] trying to understand.

—Rashida, senior consulting leader, study participant

G reat leaders build strong relationships with the people they lead, so that they can work and live to their potential. The foundation of strong relationships in the workplace is getting to know employees as individuals. In our research, we found that wellness solutions need to be tailored to employees' specific needs for them to thrive. But before you can tailor your approach to a specific employee, you have to understand who they are and what they need. It is this process of truly getting to know and seeing employees for who they are that strengthens the connection between a leader and their employees. Through this process, team members come to view their leader as more than a colleague; they view them as a confidant, or someone with whom they can share their deeper truths and concerns.

You've already learned how to set some of the groundwork for becoming a confidant. We've talked about the importance of authenticity and vulnerability. You've also learned that spending a lot of time on creating the right culture isn't always necessary; instead, we showed you how to set the right tone. Similarly, becoming a confidant should not take an enormous amount of time. Yet, too often, leaders avoid building close relationships with team members because they view it as overly time consuming. We have heard many leaders say that they would love to build close relationships with their employees but that they simply don't have the time among their other job responsibilities. Generators take a different approach. They have found shortcuts to building relationships quickly without losing meaning. This chapter will help you do the same.

Confidants Understand Employees Better

Beth, a technical specialist for a defense company, was nervous about coming out at work as transgender. She was living her authentic life outside of work, but nobody in her workplace knew her true identity. She continued to present as male at work out of fear of people's reactions. Because she didn't know for sure if their response would be supportive or unwelcoming, she didn't want to take the risk. After acquisitions and divestments that changed the shape of the company, Beth found herself working in a new town with a new leader, José. Beth and her new leader built a strong relationship right away. He quickly became a confidant. As she shared:

> [José and I] actually talked quite a bit. He worked right next to the jobs that I did. . .and we had some really good conversations. And we talked a lot outside of work, [about] things we enjoy doing. And, one day. . .he invited me to go out and eat dinner [with] him and his wife. And I said, "Well, [José], I don't look like this when I'm home in the evenings, or when I go out to eat, or anything like that." And he was like, "So?" And I said, "Well, there's not a suit and a tie. I might be wearing a dress. I'm transgender and I have been my whole life. I've known something was different since I was three or four

[years old]." And he was like, "So?" And then, needless to say, we had a long conversation that day. And then even after hours—we'd punched out, but we were still talking.

In this instance, José acted like a Generator. He showed an open mind and a curiosity to learn more about his colleague. He created a safe space for sharing information and was able to build a strong relationship with Beth by showing that he cared about her as a person. He continued doing so in the long term. Beth shared the rest of the story with us as well, which highlights even more Generator behavior from José. After initially revealing that she was transgender, instead of shying away from the conversation, José asked what would be helpful for him to know about transgender employees and how he could assist in making the workplace more inclusive. Even when learning Beth's fears about mistreatment and discrimination from colleagues José valued and liked, he listened and accepted that her experiences with them might be different from his. At the end of their conversation, she felt heard and respected, and she trusted that José would create a supportive environment.

Beth saw José as a confidant because he was willing to engage in deeper conversations that drove a more meaningful connection between them. She trusted he would be there for her and not judge her. José lived up to her expectations and used what he learned to help create a safe environment for her. As a result, she was able to come out to others at work and live more authentically. She recounted:

It kind of went from there. And actually there were four or five people on the crew that, outside of work, had met Beth and were perfectly cool with it. And they were even like, you know, "You're so much more relaxed as Beth. . ." I'm not worried about somebody finding out something [about my identity]. I just live my life.

Using the SWIFT Process

How was José able to create such a strong relationship with Beth quickly? Through our research, we were able to define a process that Generators follow to build relationships and trust faster than most leaders do. They use what we have coined the SWIFT process for cultivating connections quickly. (See Figure 5.1.) This process entails:

- **S**etting aside time for relationship-building sprints.
- **W**elcoming others warmly.
- **I**ntentionally inquiring about others' lives.
- **F**ollowing up with appropriate probing questions.
- **T**aking time to reflect for self-improvement.

As you learn about each of these steps, think about specific actions you can take to create the habit of using the SWIFT process to deepen your relationships with your team. Use Worksheet 5.1 at the end of the chapter to keep track of your identified actions.

Why the SWIFT Process Matters

Before we dive into the different steps of the SWIFT process, it's important to understand why building relationships swiftly is an important leadership goal. Think about a time when you started a new job. You likely had a lot to learn—the people, the processes, the systems, and so on. At first, it might have been hard to tell if you could trust your new boss. You might have been afraid to ask questions because you wondered if they would judge you for not knowing the answer. You might have been concerned about sharing information about your life outside of work, if you weren't sure how

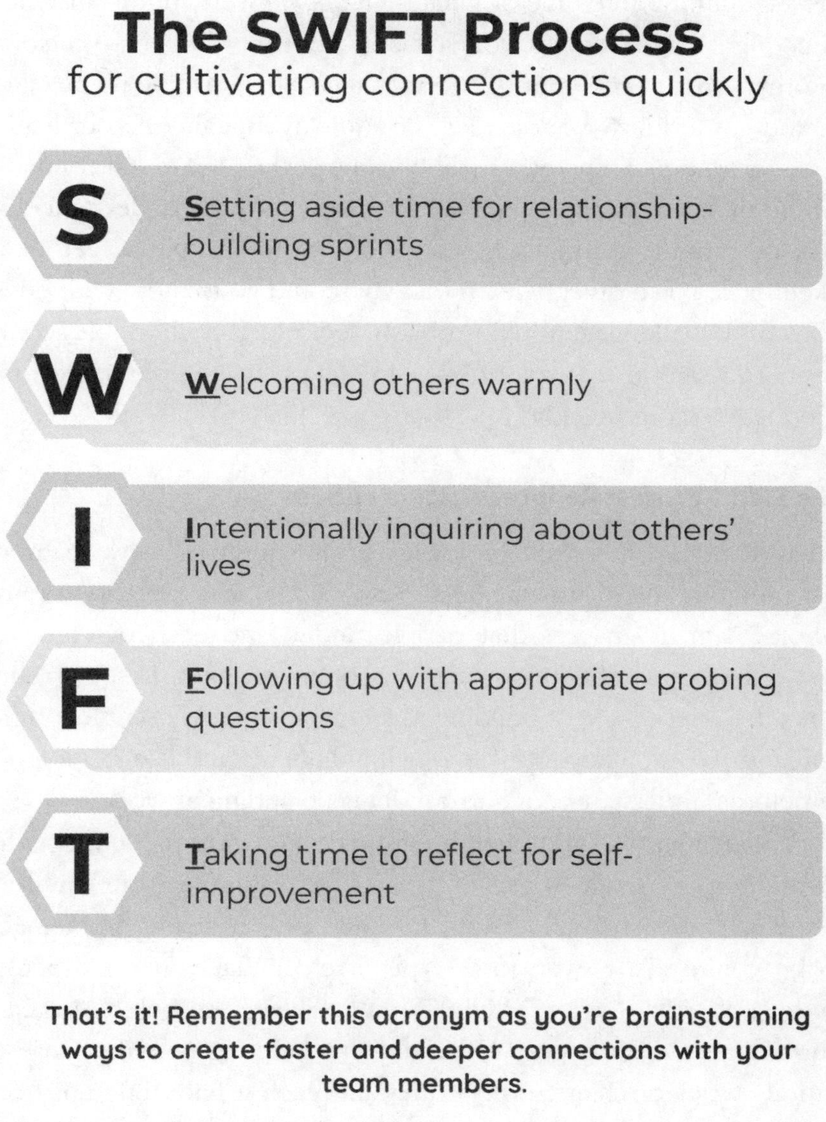

The SWIFT Process
for cultivating connections quickly

S — **S**etting aside time for relationship-building sprints

W — **W**elcoming others warmly

I — **I**ntentionally inquiring about others' lives

F — **F**ollowing up with appropriate probing questions

T — **T**aking time to reflect for self-improvement

That's it! Remember this acronym as you're brainstorming ways to create faster and deeper connections with your team members.

Figure 5.1 The SWIFT Process

they spent their free time or what their values were. In this instance, you might have kept to yourself any relevant concerns, personal information, or even your true personality. Now imagine if you came in and got to know your leader very quickly. Imagine if your leader spent extra time with you as you became acclimated to the company and to their leadership. Imagine they began to really understand you and to share more about who they were. How would that feel? In all likelihood, you'd quickly learn that you could go to them with questions and challenges. You'd probably feel more comfortable, confident, and safe in that role too—leading you to be able to become productive more quickly.

The SWIFT Process Reduces Misconceptions

In addition to helping employees acclimate to a new team or job, building swift, trusting relationships also has benefits for the whole team. It ensures that people understand each other better and reduces misconceptions and miscommunication. Research supports the importance of building relationships quickly on the job. As humans, we are likely to make quick judgments and use stereotypes to help us understand our surroundings, including at work.

This tendency can be helpful at times. For example, quick judgments help us make sense of objects or features of our environments in more organized ways. It would be extremely problematic to be confused by every new type of chair that you came across because it didn't look exactly like ones you've seen before. Instead, our brains have a category for "chair" that helps us to make sense of various types of chairs, even if they are each a little different from one another. The problem is that people are way more complicated than chairs. Making these same quick judgments about others can cause us to make erroneous assumptions that get in the way of relationship building.

Team members may make quick, inaccurate judgments about you as well. For example, if you resemble a prior boss one of your team members had, they may assume you are similar people on the inside. These snap judgments are more likely to emerge when relationships are new because you have less "individuating information"—or information that allows you to understand what makes someone unique. In the absence of information about someone's abilities, intentions, or integrity, employees will use stereotypes to make judgments about someone's trustworthiness.[1] Providing information that allows people to understand who you are as a person, your intentions, and that you are taking actions to do the right thing can minimize the likelihood that employees will use stereotypes to determine if they can trust you. Likewise, when learning about your team members, the more you know about them, the better you can suspend your own judgments.

The SWIFT Process Reduces Miscommunication

Additionally, taking time to build relationships can reduce miscommunication, especially in global or remote teams where misunderstandings are more common.[2] Spending time up front to learn about people can cut down on miscommunication. Have you ever worked with someone who sent emails that were easily misinterpreted if you didn't know them or couldn't anticipate their intended tone? In this instance, knowing more about your team member might help you understand what they mean, and it can also help you feel more comfortable coaching them to align their communications better with their intentions.

The SWIFT Process Reduces Misunderstandings

Stronger relationships also tame conflicts caused by norm violations. In other words, knowing people well helps team members assume good intentions if someone breaks team norms. Overall, when people understand more about each other, they are increasingly likely to give others the benefit of the doubt, and they will have open conversations with one another about misunderstandings.

The good news is that creating strong relationships doesn't have to take a long time. In one study, researchers Oliver Schilke and Laura Huang conducted three experiments to understand how building familiarity impacts quick relationship building.[3] They showed that providing time for participants to have a conversation before performing a task that required trust made them more accurate in their judgments about others' trustworthiness. This approach worked well regardless of whether the conversation was over the phone or in person. Specifically, people were better able to guess if their partner was behaving in a trustworthy manner on the task. The reason why this is true is because verbal contact—even without visual cues, as when you talk over the phone—allows people to see things from their conversation partner's point of view more easily. Overall, leaders building strong relationships quickly with team members has major benefits for the whole team. These relationships help new employees acclimate to the team, help team members of any tenure understand each other better, and reduce miscommunication, misunderstandings, and stereotyping overall.

Setting Aside Time for Relationship-Building Sprints

As mentioned, Generators are very intentional in making time and space to get to know their team members individually. These intentional interactions don't have to be daily or extremely long. A simple 25-minute one-on-one conversation every other week can suffice. What you do with the time is more important than the amount of time you spend doing it. As Nia, an HR employee at a small software company, shared:

I think communication, like having a weekly one-on-one with your boss, is super-important. Having that open communication, that open dialogue to talk about anything and everything, it really makes talking to your boss less stressful.

While Generators can build trust and relationships quickly, they recognize the outsized importance of their initial efforts to lay a solid foundation for new relationships. Future, shorter interactions will hold more meaning because they are rooted in an already trusting relationship. We recommend that, at the beginning of a new relationship, Generators focus on the first step in the SWIFT process: setting aside time for relationship-building sprints. Putting in more effort up front can lead to stronger relationships in the long run. Think about how this applies to other areas in life.

For example, think about a long-lasting friendship in your life. Long-lasting friendships often go through phases as life sometimes limits the amount of time you can spend together. For example, we are close friends from graduate school and we have a close-knit group of friends from that time in our lives. The group spent a lot of time bonding while we all lived and went to school together in State College, PA. Now we live in different parts of the country—yet we remain close. We were able to learn about each other in our initial interactions to a point where we can pick back up whenever we have the opportunity to get together. Or think about romantic relationships. While many established couples can happily spend a day engaging in separate activities (i.e., one person reads a book while another gardens), that agenda doesn't make for very good first date material.

Research also shows that trust in work relationships grows quicker when you build familiarity with each other and both people are able to safely be vulnerable.[4] All the work you are doing to be more authentic and vulnerable from Part I of this book will support these goals. But the key to becoming a confidant quickly is to spend time with the other person right away. Generators spend extra time to establish the relationship at the start. They inherently understand that building bonds quickly, and early, can support work relationships that are similar to long-lasting friendships. As you think about the SWIFT process, consider how you can set aside time for relationship sprints as new members join your team. It's really not that hard. You can create a new practice to have longer get-to-know-you conversations or share several meals with new employees.

We recognize that you are likely in an already established team. How can you use relationship sprints on the team today? Suddenly increasing the amount of time you spend with each employee to build relationships may feel odd and jarring to the team. Instead, pace your sprints. Don't do them all at once. Maybe lengthen one check-in a month to buy yourself a little extra time to chat. Or maybe have lunch with a different team member each week until you've gone through the whole team. Alternatively, you might consider taking a few days offsite to engage in team building. Such activities can be great for team members to get to know each other. Just ensure you also have one-on-one time with each employee in that offsite setting. As you reflect on how you can set aside time effectively for your team, take notes on Worksheet 5.1. What is one strategy you can implement this quarter that will help you schedule a few sprints of relationship building?

Welcoming Others Warmly

Now that you've set aside time to build the relationship, what do you do next? The second step in the SWIFT process is to welcome others warmly. Remember how Generators are masters at setting the tone? This is also true when they are setting the tone in their interpersonal relationships at work. They exude warmth, care, and concern

Sharing Meaningful Tokens as Reminders

Interestingly, research finds that sharing meaningful objects can help create quick relationships.[5] Specifically, an object that you gift to a team member can be a visual reminder of something you share in common and can tie you closer together. Objects can serve as symbols that are great for communicating a shared set of values or feelings. They can also connect groups together into quick, meaningful relationships.

What kinds of objects have this effect? They can be anything that you give meaning. It can be a small, framed photo of the team from your most recent offsite. Or perhaps it's a fidget spinner that you gave to an employee who shared their need to keep their hands occupied in long meetings. Or maybe each team member takes home a shell from a corporate beachside retreat. These little mementos serve as reminders of a good feeling or something meaningful that happened to you and another team member or to the whole team. We use objects as visual reminders all the time in our lives. These objects can take us back to positive memories or feelings just by looking at them.

Think of how many photos and knickknacks most folks have in their homes, to remind them of fun times or people they care about. This is why souvenirs are so popular. Objects that serve as a reminder of the bonds between work colleagues are no different in the positive impact they can make.

As you reflect on how to become a confidant for your team, think about how sharing a meaningful object with team members might support the relationships you are building.

for their employees. They are approachable and make themselves available when employees need them. Employees feel welcomed and part of the group. Research finds that leaders show warmth by demonstrating a true concern for their employees as people.[6] But how do you welcome employees warmly into your relationship?

First, take a moment to think about someone in your life whom you would describe as warm. Why would you describe them that way? Think about the things they do that make them a warm person. Warm people are typically kind, friendly, and approachable. They actively listen to what others have to say. They bring others into the group or conversation, as opposed to excluding others or treating people with a neutral attitude. Some people are naturally very warm and friendly in their approach. But not all of the Generators we heard about were those stereotypically warm people. You can welcome others warmly in ways that are *authentic* to you. In fact, it's critical that your approach is authentic to you—otherwise people will not feel the warmth but will suspect that you're faking your concern instead.

If you don't naturally have a warm demeanor, you can show others that you care with your actions. Welcoming others into their relationship with you means making yourself available. Be there for people. Make time when employees ask for help or need to chat. Keep your door open—figuratively and literally (as appropriate). You don't have to drop everything immediately when someone comes to you, but communicate and find the right time as quickly as possible. Nia, discussed previously, felt her leader was skilled at creating swift, strong connections. She shared:

> She is always available if I need to talk to her about something. If I have a question that is important to the job that I'm doing, she'll make time to talk to me that day—maybe not the minute that I sent her a message, but that day, we

will talk. That's helpful too, knowing I don't have to wait a week to talk to her about something in our one-on-ones.

Welcoming others warmly also means treating employees inclusively. Generators recognize that when in-groups and out-groups form, teams function together less effectively. So, don't play favorites. When you are building relationships, make sure you are giving all employees the chance to participate in casual conversations, meals, and important meetings. Ask their opinion. And keep them informed of what's going on around them—no one feels more excluded than when they find out information too late. We often hear from employees that leaders have their "go-to" people and leave the rest out. Assuming that there are only a few competent people on their team can become a self-fulfilling prophecy for leaders. Of course, some team members may be more talented than others, or some may excel in certain areas more than others do. Yet there are also leaders who let a mistake an employee made five years ago keep them from getting another opportunity to show their skills. Instead, these leaders keep drawing on the same handful of employees for everything—and those employees are often overworked and exhausted as a result. Ensuring that you fairly distribute opportunities and workload is important to being a Generator because it shows that you trust more than just a subset of your employees to do a good job.

Take a moment to reflect on what behaviors you can implement to be more welcoming. Can you be better at being available, especially with employees who don't know you that well? Can you do a better job of making sure you're treating employees fairly and avoiding creating in-groups and out-groups? Now go to Worksheet 5.1 and fill in the one change you will be making to welcome others more warmly.

Intentionally Inquiring About Others' Lives and Following Up with Appropriate Probing Questions

Building from welcoming behaviors, Generators ask people about themselves often and with intention. This behavior is hugely impactful in creating strong, meaningful relationships based on trust. It's not just about asking simple check-in questions, like "How are you?" Instead, it's about intentionally digging into what matters to the employee. It's about asking the right questions to get an understanding of what the employee is experiencing at work and in life (when appropriate). It's about following up and probing to understand more deeply. The "I" and the "F" in the SWIFT process go hand in hand, so we present them in the same section here.

For example, take our favorite supply chain employee, Jelisa, and her leader. Jelisa's sister was very sick, and it was taking a toll on Jelisa. Her leader had already built a swift, close relationship with her, so Jelisa felt comfortable sharing what she was going through. Yet her leader also recognized that it was important to check in to see how Jelisa was doing from time to time. This helped Jelisa to be honest about what she needed and how her sister's illness was impacting her. She recalled:

> We would talk really openly about how my sister being sick made me feel, just on the day-to-day. How was I doing on days that I knew she had to go in for her chemo treatment? Or how was I doing on days that I knew she wasn't doing any testing, but she was just kind of really run down? What did I need to do to kind of balance that out for myself? Because it wasn't just saying "My sister's sick and I feel down" but, like, "What do I need to do to try to make myself feel a little better?"

Use Caution with Your Questions

Of course, there are some questions that are off-limits legally and others that may make employees feel uncomfortable. For example, it's illegal to ask an employee whether they plan to become pregnant at some point. Follow guidance from human resources about what questions you can and can't ask your employees about their lives. Similarly, asking directly about employees' mental or physical health challenges is also off-limits. And asking employees directly about identities they may hold, such as sexual orientation or gender identity, can create unnecessary discomfort.

We recommend that, early on in your relationship, you ask broader questions about employees' work and lives, to see how you can best support them. If you allow them to reveal what they are comfortable revealing and then use that information to help better your relationship, your employees can set the pace and tone of your interactions. Some employees may not want to bring their personal lives into work, and that's okay too. Generators create an environment where employees feel comfortable sharing information that helps to improve their lives, inside and outside of work. But they also understand that forcing employees to share or asking sensitive questions directly may have negative legal or interpersonal effects.

Jelisa's leader not only asked the basic questions to check in with her during a hard time but she probed and followed up. The leader showed true concern for Jelisa's situation and wanted to understand how Jelisa was coping. Instead of feeling her leader was being overbearing, Jelisa felt seen and understood. She made it abundantly clear that her leader was an important confidante—Jelisa was able to tell her what she felt and what she needed.

In another example, Rashida, a senior consulting leader, shared that her leader was able to build meaningful relationships with his employees through his ongoing conversations in one-on-one meetings. He spent time in his conversations with the team to intentionally check in with folks and understand them better as people. She relayed:

> So I would say, for example, [my leader] had regular one-on-one meetings with his direct reports as a standard practice. And not just one-on-one meetings to be like "This is what we're working on together". . .They included both conversations about how things are going in terms of performance in general. . .but also. . ."How are things going? How are you feeling?" That regular connection point with his direct reports, of which he had seven or eight, made a place for that conversation.

Because of the relationships he built quickly through intentionally asking questions about how the team was doing, Rashida was able to open up and share about her divorce. She told us she was surprised how quickly she felt like she could open up to her leader:

> I was going through a divorce shortly after I had been hired. And for me, personally, work was a safe space at that point. And it was easy and nice to lose myself in it, and I knew I could do that well. [My leader] was very good in his [approach of] "Here's my open heart. Let's all talk about our feelings." In our one-on-ones, he's like "How are you doing?" It's amazing how some simple questions, not just performative questions, but actually asking, listening, hearing, caring—even if nobody does any actions—that was huge. I felt heard. And I knew that he cared.

Rashida's leader quickly became her confidant. She felt cared for, their relationship improved, and he was able to support her throughout a tough time.

In fact, many of our study participants raved about amazing leaders who cared about them personally. They felt supported in a way that made the workplace a safer space for them. Ada, a business partner at a global outsourcing firm, shared about her leader:

> He would start our one-on-ones, and it was all about personal stuff for the first 10 minutes. . .he knew every-thing about my life. He really got to know me personally. Whereas, I've had bosses after that where I'm like "This boss definitely doesn't know anything about my kids."

Providing a somewhat cautionary tale, a few participants also mentioned problems came along when an Extinguisher neglected to build strong relationships. For example, Finn, a data scientist at a large IT firm, described how a lack of deeper personal knowledge about a particular employee almost led their team astray:

> [We] had an employee that was not doing well, was kind of a mess and close to being fired. . .And then it was like "You've got one more shot at the company." And he had only been working for us, maybe two months. It wasn't long. Well, then, all of a sudden—like flipping a switch—he turned into a superstar, stellar employee. And I got to talking with him one day and he [told me he] had a breakup with a girlfriend and they had a kid together and everything. She was out [now]. The whole thing was over. He got that monkey off his back and he became an amaz-ing employee. And I told the manager one day, "Yeah, you know. . .he just went through a breakup." So, I couldn't

even finish my sentence, he was like "Oh, that's personal. I don't get involved in that personal life." It's like, you kind of should. Because he went from almost being fired to now being one of my best employees because of what was going on in his personal life.

Finn's peer could have been performing a lot better if the manager had supported him during a difficult situation. But because the manager chose to avoid personal topics, he almost let an employee with huge potential go. It would have been a major loss for the team. Finn couldn't believe how productive his colleague was when supported properly.

Ultimately, Generators quickly build relationships by asking about employees' lives directly and following up to understand and get more detailed information. Take a moment to reflect on how you can improve on your "I" and "F" of the SWIFT process. How can you intentionally inquire about your employees' lives and follow up with appropriate probing questions? Use Worksheet 5.1 as you start to brainstorm. Think about questions you can ask to encourage your employees to go deeper than the typical small-talk conversation. If this isn't something that comes naturally, consider writing down personal details that your employees divulge on their own, so you know what to follow up on in future conversations. On the worksheet, jot down a couple of follow-up questions that you can start practicing as you grow into your new role as a confidant.

Taking Time to Reflect for Self-Improvement

Ultimately, the SWIFT process is not linear. You will need to engage in all parts of the process continuously to build relationships quickly and to keep improving over time. The final step of the SWIFT process embodies this spirit of continuous improvement. In the other

Taking Notes Is Okay

While it may feel unnatural or forced to write down details about your employees to jog your memory, doing so can help, especially when you are starting to get to know folks or if you have a particularly large team. Eventually you won't need the notes as you get to know employees. The notes just help you as you get started with this process.

It's normal to struggle with remembering names, locations, or other details when you connect with people in a short one-on-one meeting. If your employee mentions her wife's name only every once in a while, normally just referring to her as "my wife," it'll be hard to remember what her name is. If you aren't good with names, having a written note to reference can help. And it'll make all the difference to your employee. She won't know you referred to your note but will hear you calling her wife by her name. It'll show that you are trying and caring about the details of her life.

Eventually you'll commit these details to memory, but it's okay to help yourself out a bit if you need it.

steps of the process, you've taken time to connect with your team. In this step, you take time to reflect on how you can improve. This type of reflection has been found to be important in maintaining strong relationships.[7] When you reflect on your relationships, you can grow your perspective-taking abilities and empathy toward others.

We recommend setting aside time to reflect on your relationships with your employees. Maybe it's something you do quarterly. We know some Generators who do a small reflection after each one-on-one. Ultimately, the frequency is up to you. But we recommend being intentional about your actions and ensuring you have a consistent practice of self-reflection.

Here are some points to think about in a post–one-on-one reflection. *How much do you know about this employee?*

- Do you know about their family situation? Who lives in their household?

- What does this employee like to do for fun? What are they typically doing on the weekends?

- Does this employee have a favorite food or beverage?

- What do they do to relax?

What challenges or problems is this employee facing?

- Can you tell when this employee is having a bad day or not acting like themself?

- Does this employee withdraw from you when they are struggling, or do they come to you with concerns?

Once you understand where your relationship stands, consider:

- Are you asking good questions and truly listening?

- Are you confiding in the employee as well?

- What can you do to improve your relationship?

Use Worksheet 5.1 to guide your reflections. Answering the questions about how things stand with your employees today can be a great starting point for crafting your action plans, as you take the steps identified in the first four parts of our SWIFT process. You can also revisit and revise your action plans as you learn more about your employees. What questions can you answer now that you couldn't answer before? Tracking your progress over time and updating your action plans as needed are good habits to get into.

Summing It Up

Extinguishers don't care about their employees' personal lives. They aren't interested in understanding their employees on a deeper level or in building meaningful relationships. They avoid becoming a confidant, often because they think that deeper relationship building is inappropriate for the workplace. Or they claim they don't have the time to build these relationships properly. This is a mistake. Generators know that listening to employees, understanding who they are, and being part of their support system benefits everyone. Becoming a confidant means that Generators listen and understand their team members' personal lives, while also being there to listen and understand their work-related issues. Employees intuitively tune in to this process and understand its purpose. In turn, they feel safe to share all sorts of information—good and bad—and know that their leader will be supportive in the way that they need.

To close, we share a story from Kassie, the senior consultant at a boutique firm we've introduced you to before. She perfectly summed up why becoming a confidant and probing effectively is so important:

> So I feel like there's the type of support that's like "Okay, let me know if you need anything." That's more of an empty promise of "Let me know what you need and I'll just kind of passively sit here." But with [my leader]. it's more like [she's] prompting me to identify the specific needs. . .I've been with her for nine years, so she's seen all of my growth. I think, when I was younger, I would probably go with a more vague statement about the problem— just like "I have way too much going on." And she would push me to figure out which projects were the problem and where the issues were, and work with me to get the

specific plans in place. And that has been really good. So, I think leaders helping followers to extract what their needs are and then working with them to meet those needs is a really important piece of [good leadership].

Key Takeaways

- Generators understand how to become a confidant to their employees quickly and meaningfully—leveraging the SWIFT process.

- It's important to set aside time specifically for building relationships. More time is needed at the beginning of a new relationship.

- Generators welcome others warmly onto the team and into their lives. They avoid choosing favorites.

- To truly become a confidant, you need to be intentional about asking about employees' lives and follow up with appropriate probing questions to dig deeper.

- Finally, it's important to always reflect on how you can improve your relationships with your employees. Once you've built these relationships, maintaining them is crucial.

SWIFTly Become a Confidant

As you read through each section of the SWIFT process, write down one thing you will do this quarter in each area. What small steps can you take to become a confidant to your employees?

Use the prompts for each step as you create your action plan.

S	**Setting aside time for relationship-building sprints** What is one strategy you can implement this quarter that will help you to schedule a few sprints of relationship building?
W	**Welcoming others warmly** Can you be better at being available? Can you do a better job of avoiding creating in-groups and out-groups? Identify the one change you will be making to help you welcome others more warmly.
I	**Intentionally inquiring about others' lives** Write down questions you can ask to encourage your employees to go deeper than the typical small-talk conversation.
F	**Following up with appropriate probing questions** Jot down a couple of follow-up questions to help you probe deeper when an employee opens up about personal and/or work matters.
T	**Taking time to reflect for self-improvement** Ask yourself these questions: • How much do you know about this employee? • What challenges or problems is this employee facing? • Can you tell when this employee is having a bad day or not acting like themself? • What can you do to improve your relationship?

(Continued)

Swiftly Become a Confidant

Use the space below to write down your actions.

S	
W	
I	
F	
T	

Part III

Work Should Support Life

In this part, we detail the third core component of becoming a Generator—ensuring that work is organized to support life instead of tailoring life to support work. Generators recognize that living life is of utmost importance and that their employees will not be whole people unless they are encouraged to live full lives outside of work. To do so, Generators practice two key sets of behaviors: being elastic, or recognizing that their way of doing things isn't right for everyone, and becoming "boundary bouncers," who help employees set and maintain healthy boundaries between their work and their life.

Chapter 6

Be Elastic: Your Way Isn't Always Right

I had a child the first year that I was working there and it was against company policy to work from home or to have any sort of flexibility. And my boss asked, "Why should this matter? I don't care if it's the company policy or not. You report to me. I'm the one that judges the quality of your work and if you're gonna have better quality of work by working on it at night after the baby's asleep, so be it." And I told him later, I actually had considered dropping out of the workforce because I was just having such a hard time with the guilt, [saying] "Oh, my baby's not adjusting well to day care." So both me and my husband ended up working from home one day a week so we could switch her from five days in day care to three. That accommodation allowed me to not have the stress and the guilt. [Otherwise], I was considering just leaving altogether.

—Mattie, assessment specialist, study participant

Consider the path you've taken in your career to get where you are today. What advice would you give to someone who is looking to pursue the same career goals as you did? Would you tell them your formula for success and expect they'd achieve the same results?

Leaders often think that the way they became successful will work for others if they do the same. This narrative is easy and convenient. All it requires of us is to use our own example—a sample size of one—to make generalizations about how the world works. If it works for us, we assume, it can work for them. Unfortunately, convenient narratives aren't necessarily true. The reality is much more complex. The truth is, there are vastly different formulas for success for different people. The world changes, workplaces shift, preferences and needs differ, and strategies can't always be replicated. What worked for you may not work for others. And that's okay.

Similarly, the way you like to do your work may not work for everyone either. Individual people's needs and preferences vary considerably. Generators deeply understand that their employees' preferences for how they manage work, career, and personal life vary. They also recognize that employees might be juggling different realities at home—from childcare to elder care, pet care to self-care—all of which are important to attend to but may require different approaches, effort, and time. Generators can see past their own experiences. They also recognize that the best expert on what works best for their employees are the employees themselves. Instead of criticizing their team members' approaches with tired stories about how it was "back in the day," they understand that their experience is not the only way. In turn, Generators are better able to effectively support employees' work-life balance.

Flexible Leadership Supports Employee Success

It can be hard to admit that your way isn't the "right" way or that someone else's way of approaching work might be equally as effective. Doing so requires flexibility—both in your own thinking and in your approach to leadership. Importantly, research supports the idea that people vary in their work-life ideologies—or the way that they think about how work and life fit together.[1] Lisa Leslie, a professor of management and organizations at New York University, along with her colleagues Eden King and Judith Clair, explain how employees may differ in the extent to which they see:

- Work and life as enriching each other or competing with each other
- Work and life as meshing together or as being separate domains
- Work or life as their top priority

Generators are able to embody the type of flexibility necessary to be leaders who can support these multiple and varying work ideologies.

Imagine a leader, Joann, who has been wildly successful by rigidly segmenting her work from her life. When Joann is on the clock, she is on. When she is off, she is truly off and fully away from work. Imagine that Joann sees her personal life and work life as at odds. She tries to avoid thinking about her work when she's done for the day, and she strongly dislikes when issues from home interrupt her workday. A hard worker, Joanna takes advantage of every professional development opportunity her workplace offers. But, when she is off, she completely checks out. When put in a position to choose between work and life, she feels that work is her top priority. For example, if a new work priority popped up, she would cancel time at a family event for her work.

Now imagine another highly successful leader, Matias, who is Joann's peer. Imagine he saw work and life very differently from Joann. Matias likes to mesh work and life tasks together throughout the day. He might answer emails from the sideline of his kid's soccer game or make a doctor's appointment in between Zoom calls. He prefers to shift between work and life tasks as needed. Imagine that Matias sees his work and life as complementing each other versus at odds like Joann. He was offered an opportunity to lead a committee at work but he decided to take a board seat in his community instead. Matias believes the skills he would learn in both opportunities are the same. Finally, imagine that when something new pops up at work, he chooses his family time over work. Matias will push a nonurgent deadline rather than miss a family event.

Take a moment to reflect on these two different styles. Which of these leaders are you more like? Are you similar to both in some ways? Although both of these leaders can be equally successful, it can be difficult to see how someone so different from you can reach the same level of success. Joann may feel like she works harder than Matias and may attribute his success to something else—his gender, connections, or a lenient boss. Matias may think Joann has no work-life balance and that she has to work longer hours because she's not as talented. Both of these perspectives are wrong, however. Joann and Matias both hit their goals, get results from their team, and are considered high potential in their organization. They are both great—just different in their approach. Neither way is better than the other. Just like chocolate ice cream is not inherently better than vanilla, everyone has their own way that is right for them.

Generators recognize that there are many pathways to success, and they support employees in finding ways of working that are best for them—even if those ways are different from their own. As you embark on your journey to become a Generator, you will quickly find that you have to be flexible and adaptable to allow employees to work differently while striving to obtain shared goals. Research shows that taking this approach is helpful for boosting employee engagement and productivity.[2] This may be even more true for employees from younger generations, who are more motivated to achieve a work-life balance that works for them.[3]

Segmenters and Integrators: A Key Work-Life Difference

People differ in how they want to fit work and life together. Employees usually want to either segment or integrate their work and life.[4] While employees may have different preferences for each strategy depending on the situation, generally, most people have a preference toward one or the other.

Segmenters Like to Keep Work and Life Separate

Segmenting is exactly what it sounds like—Segmenters like to separate work and life. If you are a Segmenter, you don't like it when your work time bleeds into your time outside of work, or vice versa. When one domain does bleed into the other, you are likely to feel stressed or frustrated. For example, if you are a Segmenter, you probably like to work regular hours, with relative lack of interruption, and then, at the end of the day, to disconnect and turn your attention fully to your life tasks. Work calls or emails that come in before or after work hours likely are frustrating to you. You may also feel irritated when you are forced to handle a life-related task in the middle of the workday (i.e., a child is sick, you have to sign for a package, or your significant other calls to tell you something). In other words, Segmenters like work to be work and life to be life.

Remember Asher, the leader at a tech start-up who was battling cancer? He was a Segmenter. But his leaders modeled being flexible to accommodate others' work preferences. This attitude rubbed off on him, and he started to recognize and honor others' work preferences in more nuanced ways. Their flexibility also helped him when he had to segment work from life during the workday to receive medical treatment. He shared:

111

I'm a 9:00 am to 5:00 pm person. That's just how I function. I know we have a director and she'll do some stuff really super-early, like 3:00 am to 5:00 am, and then she'll get up around noon and do some stuff. And that's fine, unless there's a meeting you just have to have and it's a customer. But for the most part, if you don't have to be on, you don't have to be on. And we just kinda know when [my coworker] is probably gonna be around and I'll ping her then. Or, if I need something, I will try to just make sure I ask her at a time when I think she's gonna be around and she'd get back to me whenever she needs to. It goes back to that whole "value the whole person" thing. I'm going to value your multiple life roles, and part of your multiple life roles may be, you have kids and you have to get them ready for school. I'm not gonna bug you while you're trying to get your kids ready for school. I'm not gonna bug you when you're picking your kids up from school. And like with me, I have so many doctors' appointments right now, people aren't gonna bug me in the middle of an appointment or they know on Tuesdays, I have to sit for six hours in a chemo chair and then after I get out I feel terrible. So Tuesdays right now people just leave me alone.

While Asher had his own preferences in how he worked, he was able to honor and respect the preferences of others. His leaders and colleagues all learned how to provide flexibility and support the various schedules and needs of their team members. Asher was able to continue being a strict Segmenter in this type of environment. While Segmenters and Integrators have different preferences, there are productive ways they can work together.

Integrators Don't Have Strict Boundaries Between Work and Life

So what exactly do Integrators prefer? Integrating is the opposite of segmenting—Integrators like to mesh their work and life realms together. Integrators don't see their lives as being split into work hours and personal hours. Instead, they view their time as fluid—everything will get done by the end of the day, but when it happens is less important. For this reason, they like to complete work and life tasks as they come and without clear separation. They also welcome interruptions more than Segmenters do. In other words, Integrators prefer work and life to happen all at once. They are comfortable with and actually enjoy bouncing back and forth between the two domains.

For example, if you are an Integrator, you might get up early and answer a couple of emails before getting your kids ready for school. After drop-off, you'll go to the office and join a few meetings. Then, after lunch, you run back to your kids' school and volunteer at a bake sale. Once you get home, you work a few more hours before eating dinner with the family. Then, after putting the kids to bed, you answer a couple final emails before disconnecting for the day. This back-and-forth between work and family responsibilities does not bother you. In fact, as an Integrator, you thrive in it. You enjoy being able to move fluidly between these various roles.

Sometimes life responsibilities turn employees into unwilling Integrators. This is not the same as having a preference for integration. Leaders can try to step in and help in these situations.

If you have an employee who's an unwilling Integrator, consider shifting their hours around. Maybe they can work in two blocks of time versus an eight-hour block with constant interruptions. Or maybe they can start working earlier in the day so that they can block time later for their non-urgent life responsibilities.

Supporting your Integrator employees can help them be happier, less stressed, and more productive. You already learned in Chapter 2 a little about Monica's experience with her leader supporting her when she had a parent going through a tough surgery. Monica, a data analyst, is an Integrator. The same leader, definitely a Generator, did a great job creating an environment where she could capitalize on her integrating preference. Monica told us about her experience:

> If you have a clear moment in your calendar and you need to step away to run an errand for an hour or two, you don't have to let anybody know you're doing that. As long as your work [performance] is doing okay, you can just step away and attend to what you need to attend to. Nobody's really asking you, "Where were you? What were you doing?" So, that's hugely supportive of wellness because it takes away some of those pressure points that you might have otherwise [experienced], in terms of how to deal with your time. It also just creates a lot more of a relaxed feeling in the organization.

Monica was able to shift between work and life tasks as it made sense to her. Doing so helped her feel less stressed and more balanced in her life. She told us how grateful she was to have the ability to do what she needed to do, when she wanted to do it.

Segmenters and Integrators Are Both Good

These two work approaches feel very different. And, depending on your preference, you may think one approach is better than the other. However, early research on segmentation and integration preferences by Blake Ashforth, a professor of management and entrepreneurship at Arizona State University, along with Glen Kreiner and Mel Fugate, demonstrated that there are pros and cons to both segmentation and integration:[5]

- While Segmenters have better boundaries between roles, they struggle with handling interruptions. For example, a phone call from a family member in the middle of the workday can be challenging for a Segmenter to handle appropriately. They may stay in "work mode" even if the family member calling needs a level of compassion or support similar to what they would normally receive at home.

- Integrators, in contrast, don't find interruptions challenging and can bounce back from them quickly. However, Integrators can have weaker role boundaries. They have a harder time carving out time just for work or just for family. It may be frustrating for family members if they are constantly checking emails instead of being more present. It can also be hard for colleagues if they will pick up any random phone call from home in the middle of a brainstorming session. This type of conflict can create challenges for Integrators that Segmenters typically don't face.

Research on Segmenters and Integrators continues to evolve, particularly as working from home is on the rise. But we are learning more clearly than ever that matching work to these preferences is critical. It's not enough just to recognize these differences. When employees are in work environments that match their preference for segmentation or integration, they are more likely to be satisfied with and committed to their work and companies.[6] Plus, they may be less likely to perceive conflict between their work and family lives.[7]

115

Keep Other Employee Differences in Mind!

It's important to note that the Segmenter-Integrator difference is not the only way that employees can differ in terms of their work preferences. For example, chronotype—whether someone is a night owl, early bird, or something in between—can also impact when and how employees do their best work.[8] The world is generally set up to favor early birds, so night owls may be forced to work in ways that make them less productive. While we won't delve into this difference between employees much further here, it is important to recognize that asking questions about work preferences and styles can help surface other important areas that employees on your team may differ on. Some questions to consider asking include:

- When do you feel most energized during the day?
- What time are you most productive in meetings?
- What types of breaks do you like to take?
- Do you sleep in on the weekends?

The more you understand your team's work preferences, the better you can support them. Plus, helping employees find their best way of working means they will do their best work. Just remember to ask these questions without judging others' answers when they are different from yours. Win-win!

Taken together, it's clear that segmentation and integration preferences for work and life impact how employees want to complete their work and their attitudes toward various work-life issues. And matching preferences to how work is done can impact employees' overall success, productivity, and happiness. Generators realize that they need to step back from their own preferences and make room for other productive ways of approaching work and life. They learn

116

their employees' preferences and help shape the environment to match.

Generators Are Flexible

While research has done a great job of showing the importance of honoring employees' preferences for segmentation versus integration, understanding how leaders might concretely create environments that match employees' needs has not yet been studied extensively. In our research, we found that Generators know how to create those environments.

Let's dig in deeper on the example that Nia, the HR employee from a small software company we discussed in previous chapters, provided. She shared how her leader was willing to proactively take steps to allow employees to adapt their workday to their preferences—including naps if needed. Nia told us that, once the pandemic hit, she really started noticing her Generator taking action to accommodate different working styles:

> At first, we were all trying to be super-professional [working virtually], wearing our office clothes while we're sitting in our bedrooms. And then all of a sudden it was like "Oh, it's okay if this coworker who's pregnant, instead of taking lunch, takes a nap, and is just completely unplugged and unavailable for that hour." I have another coworker who likes to work the eight hours straight, and so she's been encouraged to put lunch on her calendar and block that time off, like "That time belongs to you. Don't [bend] to everyone else because they're asking. Take care of yourself." I think everybody has little things like that. I know another one of my coworkers has been traveling the country with her husband and her dog in an RV but as long as she has internet access, she's good to go.

Nia also shared that her leader showed flexibility for employees who needed to manage health conditions during work hours, had recurring childcare responsibilities that cut into "normal working hours," or wanted to disconnect and take a walk during the workday. Nia's team was encouraged to block that time for themselves and take care of what they needed when they needed it.

Similarly, Julia, the VP of a government agency whom we talked about in Chapter 3, shared that her leader was willing to make accommodations for her to take maternity leave right at the start of her employment there—no questions asked and no hassles. In addition, he was also willing to accommodate her needs while she was going through a divorce and caring for her elderly father, all soon after the birth of her child. She recounted:

> The conversation [was]: "We wanna do whatever's gonna work for you." And really, that was just always the case. I think when my dad was sick, I took some leave, and I took some family leave. And then when he passed away, I took some time off. I was working [a] reduced schedule when he was in hospice, [so I could spend] time with him. But it was really just sort of "Do what you need to do," and "We're here for you." So it was just always "Okay, we're gonna make this work. So, let's now figure out how we're gonna make this work." Or there was just always the ability and the willingness to talk about "How can we make something work that the employee needs?"

Importantly, Julia's leader had never gone through these experiences himself. He didn't know how he would personally handle such situations or what he might prefer to do if he had to. But, as a Generator, he knew it didn't matter what he would do. He didn't pass

judgment and understood that being flexible with Julia was important for her ability to be happy and healthy at work. In other words,
he recognized that taking care of Julia and her work needs was the
right thing to do. Plus, it would help to retain a talented employee in
the long term—which is exactly what happened.

What About the What-Ifs?

This may all sound a bit idealistic to you and, possibly, unrealistic.
Of course you'd like to support your employees and their work and
life preferences. But what if there isn't a clear-cut way to do so? Let's
work through a couple of scenarios to help you brainstorm how to
become more like the Generators we learned about. As always, at
the end of the chapter, the worksheet (Worksheet 6.1) can help you
work through ideas on how to implement this type of flexibility.

What If Clients Make Work Inflexible?

What if you have employees who work in client-facing roles? Or
what about employees who have administrative roles that make flex
time harder to arrange? How do Generators show flexibility when
stakeholders or systems will not be as forgiving?

Kassie is a senior leader at a boutique consulting firm. We've
shared a lot of examples from her experience already in previous
chapters. She was lucky to be in a firm full of Generators. Kassie
is a great example of a person who was in a client-facing role but
still found some semblance of flexibility. Although she couldn't
structure her working hours however she wanted due to client
schedules, her leader remained flexible and amenable to schedule
changes, as long as she had some advance notice. She was willing to allow Kassie to block recurrent personal time during which
clients could not book meetings. For example, Kassie recalled a

time when she was facing childcare challenges and needed some flexibility in her schedule:

> I let my boss know I'm going to be available in a very unpredictable way. Like [my son's] going to sleep and then he's going to wake up, and I don't know when that's going to be. She was totally understanding about that. I think there are bosses who wouldn't be. . .[It helps having] a boss who will sort of give you a break when you're like "I can't be reliably responsive right now" and will just say "Okay, that's fine" or "Okay, are there any important meetings that you think you'll miss that you want to strategize about real quick?"

She also told us:

> There was a time when I was in therapy and I didn't tell my boss that I was. I was just like "Every week, I can't work for this hour." And she said okay and that was it. And I appreciate that [it was] no questions asked. . .if you can't work that hour, you [don't have to].

Although Kassie couldn't miss important client meetings without advance notice, her leader worked with her to find solutions for various challenges so that she could attend to what mattered most. As long as Kassie's leader was made aware of the challenge or situation, she was willing to find a workaround. When Kassie had a recurring commitment, her boss honored it.

Being flexible and creating an environment to support employee preferences doesn't mean there are no limits to what's possible. Generators don't dismiss business needs. They just understand how to work within the situation and balance the work that needs to be done. Most jobs cannot allow 100% flexibility. Yet Generators understand that there's always some ability to support flexibility. Further, we would never argue for accommodating someone who constantly misses meetings without warning or who shirks their work duties for non-urgent matters. That behavior falls under the umbrella of poor performance and may need to be dealt with in a different way. But for employees like Kassie, who do their job well, Generators can make a real difference by providing flexibility when possible.

What If My Company Doesn't Have Policies to Support Work-Life Balance?

Let's think about another scenario. What if you work for a company that doesn't have good policies for supporting work-life balance? What are Generators supposed to do when their organizations make it hard to be flexible? Obviously, it would be great to work for a company with inclusive, comprehensive, and flexible policies. And we would argue that if you have influence or control over these types of policies, you should do something about it. Policies matter. We know that it's not always possible to change the structure, policies, or culture you are in. Yet our study participants told us that Generators often went above and beyond what policies required to make sure they took good care of their employees' needs.

For example, Liam, an analytics manager, shared his experience with grieving a death in the family and grappling with his own personal health issues while working with an amazing Generator:

> In terms of going beyond company policy to offer emotional support that was needed—gosh, when I first started working for [my leader], I was probably working for him for [only several months] and my mother passed away. She had been terminally ill for a while—it wasn't a shock or anything like that. But just everything that was involved

121

Be Elastic: Your Way Isn't Always Right

in having to travel to the other side of the state. The company's bereavement policy wasn't fantastic. But given the circumstances that were going on, [my leader] basically said, "Take as much time as you need to deal with everything you need to deal with and I'll worry about it. Don't worry about having to log PTO or things like that. Don't worry about what the policy says." And, again, it doesn't sound like much. But it means a lot when you're in a situation like that. . .[and then] I personally had a heart attack. . .at a very young age and that was while I was working for him. And again the same thing. It was his willingness to go above and beyond what the company's policy was for dealing with stuff like that. Letting me work from home, letting me take time that did not involve me having to go on short-term disability and having to deal with all those headaches, and then just making sure that I was protected, I guess, when I did come back to work during my recovery—keeping the wolves away [i.e., making sure that coworkers didn't inundate me with emails and requests as soon as I got back].

Although the company's policies were not flexible and would not support Liam's needs, his leader decided to support him anyway. He understood that being flexible and supporting Liam was the right thing to do. Plus, Liam was still productive, meeting his goals, and, ultimately, was more committed to his leader.

This example highlights how, even in a company that lacks proper policies and structures to support work-life balance, Generators get creative. They find ways to support their employees' needs even when it's hard or requires unconventional solutions. Use Worksheet 6.1 to help you brainstorm ways to be flexible to meet employees' different work preferences and needs.

Why Being Elastic Is Fantastic

Flexibility can have a lot of benefits. We heard from our participants that they experienced a whole host of positive outcomes because of their leaders' ability to be flexible.

Retain Loyal Employees

One of the major benefits of exhibiting flexibility is retaining great employees. For example, a business partner we mentioned in the last chapter, Ada, discussed how her leader's flexibility was a primary reason she stayed with the company. She shared:

> I was at this company for about eight years, and, in that eight-year period, I got engaged, I got married, I had baby number one, and I had baby number two. As an example, breastfeeding was really important to me. Like, I pumped every single day. I was not one of those people that had a crazy amount of breast milk. . .I really had to work for it. But it was just so important to me. I could be in the pumping room all day, and no one cared where I was, because I was working at the same time, like on my computer while I was doing it. I had a babysitter where I had to pick up my kids at 4:30 pm. I had to leave at 4:00 pm and it wasn't even a question. "Go do your thing." My boss knew that I was willing to do anything for them, whether it was working at night or early in the morning, or whatever, that it was completely like "I don't care what you're doing and when you're doing it. I know you're doing it, so whatever you need to balance what's really important to you with your family, you just do it." That's why I stayed that long [there], you know?

Similarly, Sofia, a workforce health consultant, also felt that her leader's flexibility helped to retain her within her company. She noted:

> I'd say that now, as a mother, I really appreciate—of course it's inspired by the pandemic, but it will remain so, luckily—the flexibility in my schedule, the ability to work from home. Those have really changed my life in a great way because I'm able to spend more time with my family since I'm not traveling. I missed a lot when I was doing that. So that is a wellness perk or benefit that I really don't wanna go without. And if it was to be taken away I would probably seek a different position that gave me that.

Both Sofia and Ada felt grateful for the flexibility they received from their leaders. The benefit of having flexibility solidified their commitment to stay with the company and the leader who treated them so well. Who would want to leave a situation where they can be productive at work while still managing all their needs outside of work?

Build Trusting Relationships

In addition to retention, many of our study participants talked about how flexibility built trust in their relationship with their leader because it created a culture of humanity. People felt respected, cared about, and truly seen as full human beings with full lives. For example, Alba, a project manager, noted that her leader's approach to flexibility helped to cultivate trust in their relationship. She said:

> I would prefer to have a couple hours off during the day, where I can go to the gym and get that kind of stuff done and make it up later on. But that's because that works for

my schedule. And that's where I think that trust part sort of comes in with managers, where it's, like, "I know she's getting her work done. I don't really care when she does it."

Janis, an associate director of a nonprofit organization, went one step further, describing her leader's actions as driving greater humanity on her team. She enthusiastically recalled:

She understands that we're not machines and that we don't live in a vacuum. . .and actually we recently had a conversation where she's like "I'm not even married to the traditional eight-hour workday. If you can get it done in six hours, then you've gotten it done in six hours." We are going to be hybrid going forward. So, two days in the office, three days working from home. She's very supportive of that. You know, our office lease isn't cheap. And the fact that she's not going to make us be in every single day to account for that expenditure is just very, very flexible in terms of our work-life balance. And just making it easy for us to be full human beings.

Both Janis and Alba felt trusted, respected, and cared about by their leaders. They went on to discuss how these experiences strengthened their relationships with their leaders, helping them work together more effectively.

Drive Real Change

We want to end with a powerful story from Mia, the recruiting professional you met in Chapter 4. Unfortunately, Mia experienced a difficult time a few years ago. She was diagnosed with breast cancer on the same day that her father-in-law died of COVID-19. Her leader's flexibility meant the world to her as she struggled through this harrowing time. She recounted:

> Before I even had an opportunity to say "Here's what I think I'm going to need," [my boss] called me and said, "What do you need? How can I help you? What can we do?" His wife is a nurse. [He said:] "Do you want to set up a call? Do you need [recommendations for] different doctors? Don't think about work. Don't. Just do what you need to do. And you let me know what you need." And, of course, I sobbed. Because it's exactly what you want to hear from an employer. . .and so from that, as I got better and started realizing how much that impacted me, it made me realize we need to do some of these things for other people. And that's when we did a couple of blanket things of giving everyone extra PTO. But we also gave everyone the freedom to say "I'm done today. I can't do any more [work]. I'm stressed." No questions asked. Leave for the day. Do what you need to do. . . .. But it's knowing that every single day, you're taken care of, whether you have a great month or a bad month. You don't have to hit a number to be able to take care of yourself. . .whatever is important to you is important to us, so that you're a happy employee. And I think we used to be—I know we used to be—that company of the "blanket statements." And then everybody had to fit into it. [But,] it was during the last year that I think we all—[my boss] and I—sort of looked at each other and thought, I think we need to do things differently.

Mia took her experience and, in her small recruiting firm, was able to work with her leader to make broad changes. We hope that Mia's story inspires you to also do things differently. Be flexible to support people who manage work and life differently from you. Although Mia's company offered all sorts of bonuses, rewards, and recognitions, it was when her leader showed care and compassion through flexibility that he truly became a Generator.

Key Takeaways

- Generators recognize that their employees have different preferences for how to balance their work and lives.

- Preference for segmentation or integration is one of the primary ways that employees differ in how they want to manage their work and lives.

- Segmenters like to keep work and life separate, while Integrators like to merge the two domains together.

- Generators learn to create work environments to meet employees' unique needs and preferences in managing their work and lives.

- Generators earn employees' trust, make employees feel cared for, and retain their employees longer when they act in ways that honor employees' preferences and needs for managing work and life.

Worksheet 6.1

Be Elastic: Your Way Isn't Always Right

The first step in providing flexibility is through understanding your employees' work preferences. Use these next questions to start the conversation with your employees. Brainstorm your own as well.

- Are you a night owl, an early bird, or something in between?

- When do you feel most energized during the day?

- What meeting times are most productive for you?

- When do you get your best focused work done?

- What types of breaks do you like to take?

- Do you like to segment or integrate your work and life?

- Do you have to take care of certain life responsibilities during the work day?

Be Elastic: Your Way Isn't Always Right

Use this guide to help you brainstorm ways to support employees, even when policies at work aren't helpful!

What challenge is your employee facing?

Have they mentioned what type of flexibility would help them? If yes, what did they say?

Brainstorm ideas on what flexibility you can provide.

Brainstorm approaches and responses if you get pushback outside of your team.

Chapter 7

Become a Boundary Bouncer

She put those firm guidelines of, here's when I expect you guys
to be working, and here's when I don't expect you guys to be
working. And so it helps you to feel like, okay, I'm not letting
her down if I don't email her at 10 o'clock at night.

—Jelisa, supply chain employee, study participant

As we're sure you realize by now, leaders play many different roles in their employees' lives. They are guides for career development and serve as sounding boards for new ideas or solutions. They are bulldozers, removing roadblocks on the path toward success. They are mirrors, reflecting performance back to their team members to help them know where they stand. The list can go on. But the main point is that leaders—and their actions—matter in meaningful ways.

Importantly, we learned that one crucial thing that Generators do is act as boundary bouncers. A *boundary bouncer* is a leader who helps employees enforce their personal and work boundaries. Specifically, Generators don't stop at simply helping their employees set and maintain their own boundaries. They also stop other leaders who encroach on boundaries, encouraging employees to escalate boundary breaches so they can say no for them if needed. In other words, Generators use their power as leaders to push back on unreasonable expectations when employees don't feel able to. Research supports this idea, indicating that direct managers are important boundary bouncers in the workplace for employees.[1] Helping your employees manage boundaries is a critical component of your job as a leader.

A Boundary Bouncer Blocks Boundary Breakers

Our participants spoke very highly of their leaders' boundary-bouncing behaviors. Let's take Monica's story, for example. We've shared some of her experiences with her Generator already. Not only did her leader provide her with flexibility so that she could lean into her preference to integrate work and life, he also supported her in her data analyst role during a difficult time with her parent's surgery. In addition, he was a strong boundary bouncer. Monica described this type of behavior as "shielding your employee from an overly demanding or an overly aggressive client. It could be shielding them from somebody internal. . .definitely, there's an element of protection that's needed, on occasion." Monica does a great job of describing effective boundary bouncers. They help protect employees from the people around them who may breach their personal and work-related boundaries. And they are willing to do so when it's tough, such as when the person disrespecting boundaries is a client.

This same commitment to being a boundary bouncer applies to other challenging situations, such as when those breaking boundaries are more senior than the Generator. Doing this can be hard. But Generators understand that, if they can serve as a shield to employees, bad behaviors from the top will have a more limited impact. Mattie, an assessment specialist at a large media company, shared how her leader, Phil, described his role as a boundary bouncer toward other leaders in her organization. She recounted:

> [My boss] was always very open and honest with me. He said, "My job is to make sure that none of the stress, and

none of the politics and shit going on in our organization come down to you. My job is to protect you from that, to shield you from a lot of that stuff so that you can do your job to the best of your ability. I will do my best to do that."

Similarly, Alex, a marketing data analyst at a large investment firm, shared another classic example of good boundary bouncer behavior. He said:

When I was under [my boss], I would often CC him on requests that I got. Like, if somebody was emailing me, "Hey, do you think you [could get] this done?," I would often CC him. And he would kind of take the lead and say, "Hey, sorry, [Alex] is kind of booked right now. Maybe he can get to it in a couple of weeks."

We talk in Chapter 10 about some of the challenges Generators may face in absorbing boundary breakers' negative energy or inappropriate requests as well as ways to meet those challenges. For now, let's continue discussing why boundary bouncing is such an important part of being a Generator.

Employees Love Boundary Bouncers

In our research, we heard many stories about Generators engaging in effective boundary bouncing. In fact, it's one of the key things employees said they love about working for Generators. They truly appreciate feeling like their time will be protected and their boundaries respected. For example, Izzy, a recruiting manager at a large, global software company, raved about her leader for "just having [her] back." She shared:

So when it comes to more complex situations, where I'm working on a day-to-day basis with different clients or stakeholders. . .you have some managers that just have really unrealistic expectations. And so, I think for me, my wellness was also defined by how much she supported me in these challenging situations. I think that was the biggest thing.

Izzy appreciated that her leader helped set appropriate expectations with demanding clients. She also stepped in so that Izzy didn't have to say no when she didn't feel comfortable pushing back on senior leaders. Izzy told us that she felt very strongly that, without her leader supporting her boundaries, she would have burned out and had a more negative experience in her role overall. Instead of spiraling down that path, Izzy felt respected, valued, and balanced in a way that isn't typical in recruiting. Her leader benefited as well. Izzy felt a sense of loyalty toward her leader and performed her best work in that role.

Similarly, Nia, the HR employee we've talked about before, shared how her leader's boundary bouncing was a positive force in her life. She noted:

One thing is that she is very protective of our time, so if we have requests from other parts of the business and they're asking for us to build a report for them or things like that, she is very much like "How long is this going to take you? If it's taking more than a half an hour, do not do it." She's like "They can figure it out on their own." And that's pretty wonderful.

Laney, the regional director for a national educational organization we talked about in Chapter 1, discussed how much more valued and rewarded she felt when her leader supported her in setting boundaries around her work and life. In other positions, instead of being rewarded with greater flexibility for stellar performance, she was asked to work even harder. She shared:

> I really need an atmosphere that allows permission to not work, and that's not been the case. . .the more responsibility, the more projects that were sent my way, "Oh, [Laney] will do it. Not a problem." And people were not respecting the boundaries that I really needed to set. So, I feel differently at this location. In fact, my boss stopped a couple of projects that people wanted me to be involved in and [said], "No, you know, she's just getting started. She needs to learn more about the culture and get settled in with her new team before we start loading her up with other work." So that's a very different approach than what I've had in the past.

Overall, Generators fostered positive feelings about their leadership as they served as boundary bouncers for their employees. As employees felt that their boundaries were respected and valued, they gained respect for and valued their leaders more as well. They felt a greater sense of loyalty and commitment to their Generators, which led to better outcomes for everyone involved.

Boundary Bouncers Protect Themselves Too

In addition to supporting their team's boundaries, as we talked about in Chapter 4, Generators set the tone by also keeping strict boundaries for themselves—helping their team know it's okay to do it too. Research supports the idea that, when employees see their leaders as work-life role models, they are more likely to create boundaries between work and life, feel less exhausted, and be more engaged on the job.[2] For example, Laney continued her story about her new role and shared the great example her leader set in boundary bouncing for herself:

> I've only seen two people take time off since I've been here. . .one is [our leader]. And I've been working with her very closely the last six weeks because we had an acquisition that became part of my territory. And she scheduled her vacation for this week. She's on a cruise with her husband for their anniversary. A big deal. And there were some things from the project that were not quite where they needed to be. . .and she said, "We'll just take care of these when I get back. It just is what it is." And that is the way it is. Nobody said, "You really need to think about rescheduling, or could you have somebody that can [fill in]?" 'Cause it's a very lean company. We're so small. You know, "Is there somebody else that can do this for you?" They just said, "Okay, we'll wait till you get back." That's it.

Laney's leader set a strong example. She showed Laney, and others in the organization, that boundaries are important and sometimes work can wait. Laney realized that, if her leader could disconnect so fully while away, so could she. Generators recognize that they must engage in this crucial part of the process, or their efforts might ring hollow. In other words, they know that they can play boundary bouncer all day long but, if they don't show employees that they keep their own boundaries, employees will become boundary breakers themselves. For example, while Generators understand they can't physically force an employee not to check email, they recognize that if they set the example of avoiding email while away, employees will do the same.

Mia, a recruiting professional, shared another powerful example of the importance of Generators modeling boundary bouncing. In the last chapter, we talked about Mia's story in some detail. Her leader supported her and gave her flexibility during a really difficult time. Mia shared her experience with the example her leader set for maintaining boundaries, giving unspoken permission to her and her team members to do the same. She said:

> [We] try not to email outside of somewhat traditional hours. The difficulty is that the companies that we work with—they do not adhere to that. And that's very hard when a company is emailing at nine o'clock in the evening saying "I want to interview so-and-so the next morning." And so we've really tried to make an effort to say, when we are setting up interviews or engaging [with] a company. . .that we try to lay out how we work as well—not just how they work. And for our team, to see [my boss] and the leaders do that, it gives them the freedom to say to their clients "If it's after 8:00 pm, I can't guarantee that I will be able to set up an interview the next day." We're encouraging people to set their boundaries but also encouraging them to set those expectations up front.

Even in a difficult, client-facing role, Mia's leader was able to enforce strict boundaries. Generators understand that some roles may make boundary bouncing more difficult, but they work hard not to give in to typical role demands. They set expectations around boundaries early and clearly. They also stick to boundaries themselves. Without such examples, employees might feel helpless in protecting their boundaries in tough client situations. Mia's leader did a great job showing that it's okay to have boundaries and that even clients can wait, if the expectation is set from the start.

All of this sounds great, but you may be wondering how Generators operating globally and who have employees working around the clock on various projects fare at being boundary bouncers. Perhaps you are working in a global environment where work-related interruptions are possible at all hours of the day and night. For this, we come back to Mattie's experience with her leader, Phil. They worked with colleagues in Asia in a different time zone. But Mattie said that Phil set clear boundaries and expectations for her and set the example himself. She explained:

> I'm new at this role. Everyone else is answering emails. And my boss, I think one of the first weeks that he noticed me engaging in the conversations that were going back and forth, he [said], "Do not email people after dinner. No. We're not surgeons. No one's gonna die if you respond back tomorrow morning." So, the timing of emails [changed], even though for the rest of my team [the time zone was different]. I was the only person who reported to him. There were only two of us in our little work group. He was my director. The two of us would make it a point of not responding to emails at all hours of the night. He was very strict on that. He was [saying], "Don't do that unless it's something super-critical and you feel the need to. Don't bother answering anybody's emails. I don't do it, so you shouldn't do it."

Phil set an important example as a Generator. Of course, on occasion, late-night meetings or other time-zone-related inconveniences may pop up. But they should not be the norm. If everything is treated as urgent, then employees—and leaders—can never disconnect. Instead, recognizing that their jobs were not life and death, Phil told Mattie to follow his lead and stick to her boundaries.

Generators Adapt Their Boundary-Bouncing Style

We talk in the next chapter about the importance of taking a person-centered approach to leading. Specific to boundary bouncing, Generators also adapt their approach based on the employee's needs. This makes sense from a scientific perspective as well. Researchers have shown that, when a leader matches an employee's boundary needs, the employee feels more balanced and experiences less work-family conflict.[3] (Note: In the research, *work-family conflict* basically means that work encroaches on and interrupts family responsibilities and needs.)

Take Jake's situation, for example. Earlier we talked about Carlos, his leader at a major consulting firm, and how Carlos modeled the ability to disconnect, allowing Jake to feel like he could be unreachable while he enjoyed his time in nature. In addition to his evening and weekend hikes, Jake needed to take important life breaks throughout the day. He shared:

> Every day, I try to walk my dog in the middle of the day, to break up the day. Then also—we just bought a house a couple weeks ago. So, there were a lot of things we had to do. . . .I was very honest with [Carlos] that I like to preserve that time in the middle of the day but also that I have this personal stuff going on. He does a really awesome job of making me keep those other commitments that are important to my personal life. I would otherwise try to move things around to prioritize whatever we're doing on the client project.

Carlos was effective at being flexible, but he also supported Jake in his boundaries. He didn't ask Jake to shift his personal commitments around to take a meeting or do something for work. He helped enforce Jake's important boundary and ensured his boundary bouncing was aligned with Jake's needs. Boundary bouncers need to be creative in how they help support boundaries. Carlos may have other team members who don't want long midday breaks but prefer to end their workday earlier to pick up kids or catch a workout class. How Carlos boundary bounces for those employees may look different. He may work with clients to hold meetings earlier in the day with those employees and set stricter end-of-day boundaries for them, instead of blocking off the midday, as he did for Jake.

Ultimately, Generators adapt how they support boundaries to the employee's specific boundary needs. These needs can vary based on employees' personal situations, their preferences, and even the broader culture the team is embedded in.

Boundary Bouncers Encourage Integrators and Segmenters to Set Boundaries

We talked previously about the importance of recognizing employees' preferences for integration (i.e., they like to mix work and life tasks together) versus segmentation (i.e., they like to keep work and life strictly separate). Unsurprisingly, when it comes to boundaries, Generators also need to adapt to the varying needs of Integrators and Segmenters. Regarding boundaries, Integrators need more support than Segmenters. Segmenters are better able to create clear start and stop times and separate work and life when needed.[4] Boundary bouncers can help ensure that Segmenters can maintain the boundaries they set, but they usually don't need to encourage boundary creation.

Integrators, in contrast, often need help with creating boundaries. Integration may be an employee's preference, but everyone still needs a start and stop time for their work. Integrators shouldn't be integrating work and life 24 hours a day. Unfortunately, Integrators tend to neglect engaging in recovery activities after work, which leads to decreased wellness over time.[5] But Generators can help. As boundary bouncers, they not only block others who may break boundaries, but they also encourage Integrators to set boundaries and to spend time away from work. For example, Rome, a compliance manager for a transportation company, shared how his leader encouraged him to keep a weekend boundary she had set for the team. He said:

> I had a report that I needed to turn in by Friday a couple weeks ago, just before a three-day weekend. [My leader] had already told everyone earlier in the day "Hey, a three-day weekend is coming. Go ahead, everybody, take off two hours early." I said, "Hey, just to let you know, I'm behind on turning that report in." She said, "Well, if you don't turn it in by 2:00 pm, you need to leave. So, you can send it to me next week, when you get back to work." That right there—just another example of, she knows what I have going on. Sometimes you may intend on doing something by Friday, but other things happen. [Her saying] "You can turn this in after our three-day weekend" to me, that was just good for my mental health. Then it just helps build that loyalty on my part as well.

Even though Rome was suggesting he might integrate working on the report into his time off, his leader pushed him to segment instead. Rome's leader set a boundary and she expected him to keep it, even if it meant a small delay in getting the work completed. Ultimately, she understood that it was more important for him to get the rest and recovery from work that he needed than to meet an internal deadline they had set.

In another example, Calla, an account manager at a health tech company, worked for a Generator who made boundaries part of her expectations on the job, ensuring that Integrators, like Calla, didn't take their integration to an extreme. In other words, this Generator recognized that everyone needed to set healthy boundaries between work and life, and she stepped up to help the team do that. Calla told us:

> I had a review maybe a year ago. . .and she had said, "I know things are [busy]. I get it. Sometimes you're not even taking like a 20- or 30-minute break. You should be having your hour-long break every day. It's just—it's not fair. Other team members are taking their hour breaks, and the world is not going to fall apart if you do [take your break]." So she made it an objective on that review for me to take breaks. I had [another] review recently and there was [a new, tougher] objective. Sometimes you have to work late. You know, things happen. It's not the end of the world. Thankfully it's never been too bad. But she's going to reiterate it [in the comments she puts into my review] like "When you're done, you're done. You're going to [work] tomorrow. You don't have to stay extra." So that's kind of been huge because it showed that she means this. She's literally putting this on her review that she's submitting to her boss that she wants me to take more breaks or not work long hours.

Calla's leader recognized the importance of boundaries and that Calla needed time to recharge her batteries, even though she generally preferred to mix work and life together, sometimes working late into the evening hours. She didn't want to see Calla burn out and made it an explicit goal for her to prioritize her wellness in her performance review. This gave Calla the real permission she needed to step away from her work when necessary and to feel empowered to take time to truly disconnect when doing so. Both Rome and Calla worked for boundary bouncers who took their role seriously for all employees—regardless of integration or segmentation preferences. They ensured boundaries were set and held employees accountable to maintaining those boundaries.

Generators Create Boundary-Bouncing Subcultures

Moving beyond helping employees honor boundaries that are unique to them and the way they want to structure their work and life, Generators also recognize that they may need to get creative in tailoring boundary-bouncing practices to fit with their team's needs, even if the larger culture is unsupportive. Sometimes Generators are put in environments where boundary bouncing is not the norm. In these difficult situations, Generators may have to create subcultures within a larger boundary-breaking culture to support their employees' work and health happiness.[6] These leaders don't let their work context stand in the way. Let's go back to Mattie and the stories she shared about Phil. We already learned that Phil set a boundary around responding to emails in the evening. He stuck to that boundary and encouraged Mattie to stick to it as well. At times, he had to combine pushing back on more senior leaders and role-modeling boundary bouncing to preserve these practices in their microcosm of the company. Mattie shared:

> I don't think what he did was necessarily sanctioned. I know several conversations that I overheard between him and the executive director. The executive director would try to give me tasks and my boss would [say], "You work for me, not for him. I work for him. He cannot give you

tasks." And I remember when it kind of first came up and I [said], "Am I going to get in trouble for working from home?" And he said, "Let me worry about that." And he went and told the executive director, "She works for me. If you have a problem with her work output, then we'll address this." And he [said], "But don't try to interfere with anything I do with my employee."

Phil may be an extreme example, given how explicit he was with his own boss about the subculture he was trying to create. However, he was effective. He was able to protect his corner of the company from being infiltrated by broader norms that encouraged employees to break their boundaries.

Creating a subculture of boundary bouncing helps the whole team create new and effective boundaries together. Remember Part II, "It's the Tone, Not the Time"? A subculture of boundary bouncers works similarly. Team members support each other's boundaries and bring a boundary-bouncing team culture to life. For example, Chris, a program manager at a digital marketing agency, shared the ripple effects of the boundary-bouncing subculture his leader created. He noted:

> We've started to see team members put on their instant message Slack notifications the hours that they're working or give team members a heads-up when they're going to stop working each day. So, for example, we have a team member who says [she will be working] 8:00 am to 4:00 pm. And then [when] it's outside of those hours, the Slack notifications go off. She goes offline so that people know that she's not necessarily accessible during that time. That's good from a team perspective because I think that it demonstrates that people aren't working more than they should be. And that there is that sought-after work-life

balance. [It] also allows her to disconnect from work. And as a result, she has removed Slack from her phone—things like that that have made an impact. We've seen other team members then adopt and pick that up as an example of "Wow, so-and-so does this really well. What are ways that I can kind of emulate that and make sure that that's a part of my life too?"

Generators understand that even when the broader environment is not fully supportive, creating the right team culture, even if it pertains only to their own team, can make a huge difference in employees' lives. Plus, it takes away some of the pressure from being the sole boundary bouncer on a team. Yes, Generators may be critical in protecting the team from other leaders. But they don't have to be the team's only internal shield. A boundary-bouncing subculture ensures that team members don't become boundary breakers for each other. Rather, the subculture supports everyone playing the part of boundary bouncers within their bubble.

Sometimes creating a subculture means that you don't have a boundary bouncer supporting you from the top. It can be hard to be the shield if you are getting a lot of work dumped on you. If this sounds like your situation, we recommend finding partners throughout the organization. Where are your fellow boundary bouncers? Are there like-minded peers in your company? Recruit them to the boundary-bouncing team and slowly start a movement. Leverage each other to practice saying no. Help play boundary bouncer for each other. As you find other boundary bouncers and band together, you can slowly shift the overall culture, not just your own subculture. We discuss this in more detail in Chapter 10.

Practice Boundary Bouncing

Take a moment to reflect and think about how you have been a boundary bouncer in the past. Also think about how you may have been a boundary breaker, either by breaking your own boundaries or by encroaching on others' boundaries. Use Worksheet 7.1 at the end of the chapter to capture your reflections.

Next, take some time to consider how you can strengthen your boundary-bouncing practice. Breaking old habits can be hard. If you've generally embraced the mentality that work should take precedence over life and that a work issue interrupting personal time always needs immediate attention, it can be hard to stop boundary breaking. Consider these questions:

- How did you come to learn that boundaries are meant to be broken instead of respected?

- Who was an early role model who showed you that was the right way to work? Perhaps it was a parent or a formative boss.

Sometimes it is helpful to recognize where our expectations for ourselves and others come from. Recognizing that some of what you believe to be the most effective ways of working is based on norms that you learned makes it easier to reset your internal monologue and mindset about the value of boundaries.

Sometimes we just accept the norms around us without really thinking about whether we like them or if they are working for us. If you would prefer to have stronger boundaries between work and life, think about how your own expectations for yourself might play into the patterns you exhibit versus your preferences. Maybe others' expectations for you are the issue. Consider these questions:

- Can you create a subculture for yourself and your team where things are done differently?

- Will you get pushback for doing things differently or do you just imagine you might?

Perhaps your new way of respecting boundaries will be hard for others to adjust to at first. But eventually they will give in when they see your team is still productive. The bottom line is that it's important to recognize your own norms and expectations about boundaries, for yourself and others, and to question whether they are the norms you really want to uphold or just others' norms you've inherited. If you don't want to be a boundary breaker, you can change and do things your own way.

If that's the case, you'll need to be vigilant as you make the switch toward enacting this key Generator behavior. As you start to take action to set your own boundaries and to help others to set and maintain theirs, pay attention to the context when things don't go as planned. Consider these questions:

- What are the challenges you come across?

- What circumstances cause you to break a boundary or lack respect for others' boundaries?

- How can you avoid those circumstances, or navigate them differently, in the future?

- It's also good to keep track of who causes you to break boundaries. Who are the boundary breakers in your organization?

- How can you handle their requests differently?

- How can you convince those individuals of the value of the new practices you're trying to instill?

Begin brainstorming ideas on how to protect yourself and your team by blocking those boundary breakers.

Finally, consider explicitly what boundaries you want to set and have open conversations about what boundaries your team members would appreciate strengthening. If you don't have many clear boundaries right now, dedicate time to think about what you want your boundaries to be. Bring a list to the team and discuss their boundaries as well. Create a shared document where everyone can see each other's boundaries and begin creating a subculture of boundary bouncers. Given the way the world of work operates, doing this may be tough. But Generators are successful because they go against the grain, in a good way. You can too. Remember that this effort might require some extra mindfulness about disrupting your current boundary-related habits and norms and replacing them with new ones.

Key Takeaways

- Generators are boundary bouncers. They block employees from people or situations that violate their boundaries.

- Boundary bouncers also protect their own boundaries and lead by example.

- Boundary bouncers understand that they need to adapt how they protect employees' boundaries based on their employees' unique needs and preferences.

- Boundary bouncers go beyond respecting their own boundaries by also helping employees set and maintain boundaries, if they struggle to do so themselves.

Become a Boundary Bouncer

Take a moment to reflect on how you've dealt with boundaries in the past. When have you been a boundary bouncer? When were you a boundary breaker?

As you review your answers, reflect on why you did or did not succeed in the situation to support boundaries.

When have you been a good boundary bouncer for your team?
When have you been a good boundary bouncer for yourself?
When have you encroached on others' boundaries?
When did you break your own boundaries?

(Continued)

Become a Boundary Bouncer

Now let's begin planning on how to become a better boundary bouncer. First, brainstorm challenges and ways to overcome them. Then define your own boundaries to share with your team.

What challenges do you face in protecting boundaries?
Do you have any boundary breakers in your company? Who?
Brainstorm a few ideas on how you can overcome these challenges.
Create a list of your own boundaries that you want to protect.

Part IV

One Size Doesn't Fit All

In this part, we discuss the final set of behaviors that Generators engage in—demonstrating that wellness solutions aren't one size fits all. Generators value the diversity of their employees' needs and desires and work with them to create plans for success at work that support their overall wellness. Generators uncover and provide effective solutions for employees' specific wellness struggles through person-centered planning and destigmatizing mental health challenges.

Chapter 8

The Power of Person-Centered Planning

I was completely burned out and absolutely miserable [at the end of a challenging assignment]. They wanted to throw me into a different assignment right away. I called [my Generator] and I told her that I was broken, and that I thought I was gonna quit. I was just gonna walk away without having anything [else lined up] because I was so drained. She was just like "If you could do anything, what would you do?" I was like "I don't know. Send me on a short assignment anywhere. Just give me the exact opposite of what I'm doing for a little while." She was like "Let me get back to you." Two weeks later, she calls me back and she's like "What do you think about an international assignment. . .with a completely different business unit doing the complete opposite of what you're doing here? Right now, you've shut down [a] facility. You've done massive layoffs and restructuring. How about helping build up a new business in [another country] for a couple of months?". . .Wellness doesn't look the same for everybody, right?

—Carly, senior HR manager, study participant

Generators recognize and act on the idea that one size doesn't fit all when it comes to wellness. You've already learned the importance of flexibility and how employees may have different needs and preferences in how they work. Part III was all about how work should be tailored to help support life. In this chapter, you will go even deeper and learn the advanced skill of person-centered planning—bringing to life the idea that one size doesn't fit all.

Taking a one-size-doesn't-fit-all approach requires both a mindset shift and a set of behaviors that help you execute on the mindset shift successfully. As a leader, it's important to recognize that your needs and wants are not going to be the same as others'—and that's okay. Just as you may be an Integrator and you have to flex to support your Segmenter team members, you may need to think about wellness strategies in ways that depart from your own conceptualization of wellness. To provide employees with wellness solutions that actually work for them, you need to tailor them to their unique needs, preferences, and struggles. Doing this requires a commitment to *person-centered planning*, which we unpack in this chapter.

Generators practice person-centered planning as they work with team members to address their unique wellness needs. This planning process involves three core steps:

1. Provoking honest and transparent responses
2. Suspending judgment
3. Showing empathy

These core steps are important, both as you gather information and insights from your employees and as you conduct action planning on what to do to support them.

Person-centered planning is a natural next step in your skill development as a Generator. You'll be building on skills that you've already learned from prior chapters, elevating your growth. All of our strategies thus far have helped to bring you closer to your team members. In particular, person-centered planning leverages the skills you've built to become more authentic with your employees and the SWIFT process you're using to create quick but deep relationships with others at work. When you are already showing your authentic self to others at work and your relationships are deeper than surface level, gathering the information needed for this type of planning is much easier. With the appropriate insights, you can prepare for the future and put each employee at the center of their own planning process.

How do you gain these insights? Directly from your employees! Because you've built meaningful, authentic relationships with them, employees are more likely to be honest with you about what they need. In turn, you can both be candid about possible solutions. Generators sometimes have to work creatively within systems to find solutions that meet employees' needs. And, at times, being candid can require Generators to be transparent about the limitations of the organizations that they are working within and a willingness to think outside the box to find a workable solution. Because this chapter represents a true "level up" in your skillset, if you aren't feeling solid about the skills you've gained in the first three parts of the book, we encourage you to revisit them before diving in here.

As you begin to learn about person-centered planning, it's important to note one thing. Crucial to planning in a person-centered way is setting aside intentional time to discuss how your employees are doing and what they currently need. Doing this requires an investment of your time up front—just like so many of the strategies you've learned thus far. You need to spend dedicated time with employees, to ensure that you fully hear and learn from them about their needs. This up-front time investment will pay off down the line. You'll eventually be able to gauge and adapt to your employees' needs on the spot. We know you are already busy—and we're asking you to work on developing several new skills to become a Generator. But we urge you to not let that discourage you or get in the way of your open-mindedness about engaging in these strategies. In Chapter 11, we help you build an action plan that breaks these strategies down into smaller, more manageable chunks. And, remember, while it may take some additional time to develop these skills, becoming a Generator will save you time and stress in the long run. As a Generator, you'll have a committed and healthy team, working happily alongside you to achieve team goals.

Person-Centered Planning: A Rogerian Approach

In our research, participants shared many examples and stories about how Generators engaged in person-centered planning. As we were digging into our data, we also looked to other scientific research to understand what Generators were doing and why it was so effective. We quickly realized that Generators' behaviors were aligned closely with an existing approach to strengthening relationships in general, not just in the workplace. Specifically, a classical approach to engaging in therapeutic dialogue with others from the 1960s, rooted in the work of Carl Rogers, award-winning psychologist and a primary founder of humanistic psychology, matched the stories participants were sharing.[1] While this Rogerian approach is decades old, it remains popular because of its powerful impact.[2]

The *Rogerian approach*, as used by therapists, puts the client at the center of the dialogue. This approach asserts that people can fully flourish only if they are able to work through challenges with someone who values them as a person and who connects with them in a way that allows for their humanity to shine through.[3] People need to feel fully understood by trusted others when sharing their needs. These trusted others can then help people to create effective action plans and provide guidance that really works, because the guidance resonates on a deeper level. In our conversations with study participants, we learned that this approach is also impactful in a setting different from the classical approach: at work with leaders.

The Rogerian approach requires some initial groundwork to achieve positive end results. Importantly, this approach means showing unconditional regard for another person's self-worth. Even if what employees share with you is tough to hear, or isn't something you have experienced, you have to maintain your support for their value as a person and as a colleague. Let's consider an example. Marta is a leader who is naturally very organized at work. One day her employee, Ollie, shares that he is struggling with staying organized. Her initial reaction might be to think "that's silly" or "something is wrong with Ollie if he can't understand something as simple as staying organized." However, taking a Rogerian approach, Marta listens carefully and puts her judgments aside. She reframes the situation with a reminder that she also has shortcomings that others may not have. She maintains Ollie's self-worth, meaning she believes he is a worthy, valuable person, and she accepts him fully for who he is.

When you engage in dialogue that preserves others' self-worth, you open yourself up to better understand how they are feeling. You can put yourself in their shoes. If you are judging them or disregarding their self-worth, you create mental barriers that block you from feeling what they are feeling and seeing the world from their point of view. Consider the mindset shift that Marta undergoes when she moves from thinking "that's a silly concern" to "that isn't something I've struggled with, but I can imagine times that I have struggled with something in a similar way and feel for this person because I know that's tough."

Importantly, when employees have conversations with you that preserve their self-worth, they feel seen, heard, validated, and supported for who they really are and thus are better able to live out their full potential. They feel permission to authentically be themselves, growing more confident and feeling more competent over time. In Rogerian terms, employees who are treated with a high regard for their self-worth can become "fully functioning," or happy and well. The relationship between person-centered planning and wellness is direct—just being a part of this process boosts employee wellness.

The Rogerian Approach Empowers Employees

As with other Generator strategies we've suggested, one of the best parts about the Rogerian approach is that it ultimately saves leaders time. This is because the Rogerian approach empowers employees to recognize that their feelings and thoughts are valid and worthy. This person-centered approach shifts the focus of trust to employees because leaders show that they trust employees to understand what they need to thrive.[4]

By valuing employees' perspectives and validating their worth, you show that they know better about what's best for them than you do. Over time, employees feel empowered to overcome challenges themselves or come to you with possible solutions instead of merely coming to you with problems. Even better, when you show empathy toward what employees share with you, you provide a safe space for them to create their own career or life plans that resonate with who they are—not who you think they should be. Over time, this process helps shift employees' mentality toward you—they now see you as a sounding board rather than as a personal problem solver. It takes leaders less time to hear an employee's concerns and partner with them to find a solution than to constantly put out fires or solve everyone's problems for them. For these reasons, taking a Rogerian approach is a more efficient way to lead.

The Rogerian approach can be difficult as a leader because it goes against the norms of what many think it takes to be a good leader—being tough, calculating, unfeeling, and unattached. Recognizing that the typical, competitive workplace dynamics that have dominated organizations for decades miss the point requires a mindset shift. Generators recognize that these outdated ways of leading prevent them from really seeing people as people instead of just workers.[5] The mindset shift required for person-centered planning requires letting go of the idea that people are productivity machines whose only value is their ability to deliver results. It's a shift toward the idea that employees are humans first and that they are valuable regardless of their status at work. This step is not only crucial toward becoming a Generator, but it's also critical in reversing the damage done by these traditional narratives, which have made employees feel more like cogs in a machine rather than whole, valued people.

When leaders make this shift, employees put away their masks.[6] They start to find solutions that will work for them. When employees don't feel valued as whole people and don't sense empathy from their leader, the solutions they create will be less effective, following more normative guidelines that don't align with the real problems they are facing. Thus, person-centered planning also saves time and energy because employees suggest solutions that are much more likely to be effective.

Let's go back to Ollie and Marta. If Marta wasn't practicing the Rogerian approach, Ollie might feel embarrassed by his shortcomings. He might avoid being truthful about his struggles and may try to handle them privately. Since Marta doesn't understand the root cause of Ollie's challenges, when Ollie is late on delivering something or has errors in his work, Marta may provide the feedback that he should engage in the same strategies she uses to make sure her work is done well and on time. Seeing these are the strategies Marta prefers, Ollie falls in line with them. However, these solutions don't address Ollie's struggles with staying organized. They don't fix the problem from the bottom up.

Let's think about how the situation might look different if Marta practiced the Rogerian approach. Now Ollie is honest about his struggles with staying organized. He may come to Marta asking for a specific software tool that can help him stay more organized. Marta now has a solution she can work on with Ollie to help address the root problem, not just the symptom.

Although the Rogerian approach was created outside of the workplace, it has been shown to be effective in a variety of contexts. For example, it has been shown to improve community relations with police in Canada.[7] When police engaged in community-centered planning, people trusted them more and their relationships improved. Elite athletes also have shown improvements in their ability to perform when they are coached in a person-centered way.[8]

Related research has studied many of the same principles as the Rogerian approach. Specifically, research supports the idea that leaders with better social intelligence are more effective.[9] Aligned with person-centered planning, social intelligence includes the ability to solve complex problems by leveraging other people's perspectives.

> The Rogerian approach reflects a shift toward the idea that employees are humans first and that they are valuable regardless of their work status or rank.

Although we weren't studying the Rogerian approach directly, our research supports the basic principles. Our participants spoke of Generators who followed the basic three steps of person-centered planning. Thus, we are confident that engaging in a similar process with your employees will yield positive results—for them, for you, and for your organization.

The Three Steps of Person-Centered Planning

Based on the Rogerian approach, leaders hoping to become Generators should engage in the three-step process of person-centered planning. Again, these core steps are:

1. Provoking honest and transparent responses

2. Suspending judgment

3. Showing empathy

> Setting aside intentional time to discuss how your employees are doing and what they currently need is critical to planning in a person-centered way.

The next subsections look at each step in detail.

Provoking Honest and Transparent Responses

First, let's focus on provoking honest and transparent responses. When employees feel safe talking to you, they can provide honest responses to your inquiries. Their responses are more likely to contain all the relevant information and details you need to help support their wellness and productivity. To elicit honest responses successfully, you need to engage in a few key behaviors:

- When meeting with employees, make sure that you are in a comfortable space that doesn't reinforce power or hierarchies. For example, if you meet in your office, you might be behind your desk and the employee might be on the other side. While that may work in some instances, coming out from behind the desk and sitting across from an employee, or at a round table, might signal that you are equals in the conversation.

- Let employees know up front that you are interested in hearing their candid thoughts and are entering the conversation without judgment. Sometimes leaders think their intentions are clear, but they aren't communicating them directly. Telling your employees your intentions for the conversation can ensure that your intent doesn't get lost in translation.

- You can ask employees what you might do to make the conversation more comfortable. For example, perhaps the walls in your office are thin and an employee doesn't feel comfortable sharing freely because others might hear. You might meet with that employee in a different location where they feel freer to share.

The bottom line is that employees need to feel safe and valued as they enter into dialogue with you. You can make those feelings more likely by asking what they need and by expressing your intentions directly.

Consider how you may start implementing these behaviors. Use Worksheet 8.1 at the end of the chapter to start brainstorming how to create a more comfortable environment for your employees to engage in honest dialogue.

Suspending Judgment

As you are engaging in dialogue, suspending your judgments about what is being shared with you is vital. Using your own perspective to decide what is normal or acceptable is easy. But we are all different, and it's important to keep in mind that your "normal" may not be someone else's. In other words, just because something is aligned with your way of thinking or behaving doesn't mean it's the best way—or even the typical way—compared to others' thoughts and behaviors.

Additionally, as employees talk to you, it's important to practice active listening. Make appropriate eye contact. Show that you're listening by affirming what they are saying or by stating back what you heard. Genuine statements like these can go a long way:

- "I haven't personally experienced what you're describing, but I'm hearing that you're struggling, and I can understand what that might feel like."

- "What you're sharing is very valuable and I'm glad that you're bringing it up. This sounds difficult and I'm glad we can now work together to brainstorm solutions."

In other words, even if you haven't shared a struggle that an employee is having or if you have judged those with the same struggles in the past, you can shift your behavior to suspend judgment now. Generators don't judge. They listen, learn, and use information as an input for creating solid, effective solutions when employees face challenges.

Use Worksheet 8.1 to reflect on times you've battled the urge to judge others as they share struggles and challenges. How can you better suspend your judgment?

Showing Empathy

Finally, person-centered planning requires empathy. Sometimes people confuse *sympathy* and *empathy*. Sympathy is a feeling you have when you feel bad *for* another person. Empathy is experienced when you feel emotions *with* another person.

Sympathy creates distance between people because it doesn't require truly putting yourself in another person's shoes. Understanding that someone is going through something tough and feeling bad for them is not the same as sitting down with someone and vicariously living through their struggles. Generators don't just say "I'm

163

The Power of Person-Centered Planning

sorry you're experiencing that." Instead they say, "I am really striving to understand your feelings and am trying to view the world through your lens so I can feel how you feel and see things how you see them." Empathy can make a big difference to employees. When employees feel that your responses are empathetic, they recognize that you are in tune with their emotions and thoughts. Empathetic responses make them feel safer sharing the truth and coming up with solutions that resonate with reality and what they need to improve the situation.

Use Worksheet 8.1 to reflect on your current level of empathy. Is it easy for you to step into someone else's shoes? If not, how can you practice taking others' perspectives?

Following these three steps will help you create an environment that employees view as safe, that promotes their feeling valued and supported, and that bonds you together as a team when problem-solving. In contrast, Extinguishers ask employees to engage in dialogue in ways that suit their own preferences (but perhaps not the employee's), discard or degrade the way employees feel or think, and keep employees at a distance in the problem-solving process. When put that way, it's easy to see why person-centered planning is preferred to other methods of solving employees' wellness concerns.

The Three Steps to Person-Centered Planning

1. Provoking honest and transparent responses

2. Suspending judgment

3. Showing empathy

When you engage in these three key steps, employees feel safer sharing their true struggles with you. They are also more likely to

---

feel supported and valued. In the long term, they are empowered to tell you honestly what they are challenged with and to come up with possible solutions to these issues on their own. You no longer need to be a firefighter, or the first line of defense for single-handedly solving employee issues, which are also more likely to crop up again because they haven't been addressed at the root.

This is why person-centered planning is better for both employees and Generators.

Why Is Person-Centered Planning Important?

Our participants shared with us that person-centered planning was core to how Generators ensured that their employees' wellness needs were being met at work. The Generators' actions created safe spaces for participants to share their struggles and needs. Participants felt that their Generators were nonjudgmental and empathetic to the challenges they faced, which created a workplace where they felt happier, healthier, and more productive. This is the "why" of person-centered planning.

For Jelisa, the supply chain employee from prior chapters, being able to share safely with her leader about an issue completely changed her work experience. She was having chronic migraines, triggered by lights in a major conference room they used for meetings and to complete group project work. Being heard and supported by her Generator was crucial to promoting her wellness and productivity. Jelisa shared:

> She just had a way of knowing what you needed and taking care of that without bringing attention to it. . .The biggest part for me was, I would always avoid volunteering

to be a part of things if I knew that [it] would include having to be in the conference room for a long period of time. Because the lights were a big problem for me. I was always just afraid [that] if I go in there, it's [going to] cause me to have a migraine. Or I'm going to go in there and my anxiety's going to start to increase, because I'm going to start feeling the pain. . .After her and I had that conversation [about my issues with the lights], she invited me to a meeting and she said, "Come on, let's go." And I just went with her, thinking "Oh my gosh, I'll tough it out". . .but we got in there and she dimmed out one of the lights. Imagine four light switches and she turned off every other one. And she didn't make a point about it. She didn't bring any acknowledgment to it. She just did it and went and sat down, and I came and sat down with her. And nobody said anything. She just kind of showed me that my fear was more internal than it was actually external. . .and it also made it much easier for me because then we didn't have to have that conversation [in the larger group]. She didn't point it out. It wasn't like a big thing. And so the next time I had to go into the room, I did it myself. And the same thing happened. Nobody responded. Everything was fine.

Later, Jelisa's leader went a step further to obtain additional resources that might help. Jelisa shared:

She said, "Hey, I've been looking around at stuff that I needed to get for my office. And I found these lamps. We could get you one. We could put it over here in the corner and that way you wouldn't have to leave this light on." And so it was just like—she did the work. She found that. She said, "This would be great." And so then we got it.

The company paid for it. We brought it in and it helped tremendously because it had a different light bulb in it. So like there's a difference between LED lights and the lights that you have at your office. It puts off a hum that really bothers people with migraines. And she did actually look and this lamp didn't have that. It had the LED light bulb, so it wasn't putting off that same thing. But again, it was not something that she made a big deal about. And I think that has always been such a huge thing for me in not wanting to feel different from everybody [like I'm a] problem or I'm a burden. And so for her just being like "I was doing this and I saw it and I thought of you." It was really helpful.

Jelisa's leader practiced person-centered planning by listening to her employee's issue, not judging it, showing empathy, and finding a reasonable solution. Unlike the Generator who asked Jelisa about her behaviors, an Extinguisher may have made their own judgments about why Jelisa was avoiding the conference room or seemed stressed or exhausted after long meetings there. Instead, her Generator took time to understand the truth. She deeply understood the problem and supported Jelisa effectively.

In another example, Monica, the data analyst at a large retailer, mentioned that her Generator paid attention to what would make her happiest and healthiest in her life outside of work. For Monica, this meant living closer to her hometown. Especially during the pandemic, she was feeling lonely living on a different coast from her family and friends. Her Generator helped support her move, without hesitation or judgment, and with empathy for her needs. This attitude was in stark contrast to a prior job in which Monica's needs were overlooked and treated as unimportant by an Extinguisher. She shared:

The fact that they made it so freaking easy for me to move was hugely supportive. . .they just wanted me to be more satisfied in my personal life, and they kind of pushed for that to happen. And so that was definitely a hugely supportive move. When I worked for my [prior company]...my boss lived in [the Midwest], so she was working remotely. And I was living in [the South]. And I had, at one point, asked her if it would be possible to move to [the West Coast], because she was already remote. So, it's not like we saw each other every day anyway. And she flat out said, "No. Never going to happen." Yeah, so that's actually why I left the company, that's why I ended up looking for other jobs, because I was, like "I'm tired of living here, and I know I'm not gonna have the option to work elsewhere. Might as well start looking outside the company." And also, if she hadn't outright just said no and closed the conversation down—like, if she said, "Well, the way things are currently working out, I wouldn't be allowed to do that," because at a massive corporation like [prior employer], there are all kinds of rules. Like, it's entirely possible she couldn't have made me remote even if she wanted to. But if she just said that and then said, "Why don't you put in a couple years here, and then we'll see about that. Maybe I'll try and help you find something [on the West Coast]," or, "I'll connect you to somebody out there in a different position and we'll work on getting you out there." That would've been a different ball game. But that's not what she said.

Monica, just like most employees, is not unreasonable. She understood that not all things are possible. However, a Generator taking a person-centered approach made all the difference for her. Luckily, things worked out well for her move. But, even if the ideal solution wasn't possible, Monica would have respected and appreciated a person-centered approach to her challenge—and not a dismissal or a judgment, as she had received from her previous leader.

Finally, Olivia—a senior consultant at a major consulting and research firm—told us about her experience deciding to share with Generators about her struggles with ADHD. Her leaders' willingness to listen and learn from employees' experiences with neurodiversity helped her to feel more comfortable sharing her struggles and helped the leaders come up with solutions that fit the challenges she and others were facing. Paying it forward, when she saw a similar issue on her own team, she was able to be a Generator to another team member struggling with dyslexia. In her company, Olivia felt that Generators made all the difference in the health, well-being, and performance of neurodivergent employees at work. She shared:

> I have pretty complex ADHD and have dealt with it my entire adult life. I've noticed that a lot of employers haven't been thinking about people who aren't neurotypical when talking about wellness. . .they're not thinking that my brain might be working a little bit differently than other people that I might work with. So, where I work right now, there's been a push in the last year or so to start addressing this. We've had panels for our leadership teams where people come in and talk about what this means from a job design perspective and a person perspective. So I know it's on the radar of my current organization. One thing that I think has been a little difficult with this particular topic has to do with medical privacy. A topic that came up a lot on quite a few panels and surveys is that people aren't necessarily comfortable talking to their managers if they're dyslexic or they have ADHD or something along those lines. So it's

important for a company to tailor or have a good approach where people are comfortable talking about it in the first place. . .I've even noticed that my work, the more that people are actually talking about it, the more panels that we've had. . .it's just interesting how many people who are so advanced in their career have never come across this before or even knew that they had people that had issues with some of this. I think just communicating about what it is and how it's okay [helps]. . .I did have an employee once who had dyslexia and they didn't report it. And what was happening is, on performance evaluations, like when this person's performance gets evaluated every quarter, we were getting some feedback from clients [that] mistakes were being made on reports and just basic things. And it looked like this person was just sloppy. Nobody had any idea that they had a learning disability. And it took them like a year to even be brave enough to say "Hey, I struggle with this." And so, even equipping leaders to be able to have that conversation and just not making an assumption that somebody's lazy or they don't want to do a good job, but "Hey, this is unusual for somebody who has a master's degree to be making these kinds of errors. Maybe I need to dig in and figure out what's going on."

In Olivia's situation, once leaders took a person-centered approach, the conversation shifted to one without judgment and with empathy. It allowed for solutions to be co-created that helped everyone thrive and succeed.

In all these examples, Generators were willing to listen and learn from employees about their unique needs, even if they differed from their own. They created safe spaces for sharing and allowed employees to share without fear of judgment. Then, leveraging their empathy for their employees' situations, they derived solutions that supported their health and happiness. All of this helped employees perform better because they truly *felt* better, through the power of person-centered planning.

Generators Recognize that Breaking Bad Is Sometimes Good

You may have noticed that, at times and when appropriate, Generators go above and beyond the rules and regulations of their organizations. They understand when it's necessary to create effective strategies for solving the problems they learned about through person-centered planning. Jelisa's leader simply went ahead and changed the lighting in the conference room to accommodate Jelisa's needs. Monica's leader worked to help her relocate, even though that wasn't the norm for the company.

It may not always be possible or wise to bend the rules, but Generators know that sometimes rules need to be challenged. More specifically, Generators are willing to take matters into their own hands to provide employees with what they need. If you are feeling resistant to an employee's request, ask yourself some key questions:

- Are you feeling resistant because what they are asking for is not aligned with company norms? Consider, instead, if what they are asking for is still possible, even if it's not the norm.

- Are you feeling resistant because you've been told *no* in the past for a similar request? Consider whether the people involved or culture of the organization has shifted since that original request.

- Are you feeling resistant because you have never needed similar resources at work? Consider why you think a difference in needs between you and the employee is blocking you from helping them.

If the answer to any of these three questions is yes, you might want to explore whether your resistance is due to an actual, real inability to provide a solution. Or is it possible that you are simply unwilling to go to bat for an employee or to honor their concerns as legitimate?

We talk further about challenges Generators face in Chapter 10, including other people who may serve as roadblocks in your way to being a Generator (i.e., gatekeepers who reject your solutions for supporting employee wellness). For now, we ask that you carefully consider how your own reactions to employees' wellness concerns might drive your motivation toward resolving them. Consider whether these motivations are driven by judgment or a lack of empathy—the enemies of an effective person-centered planning process.

Key Takeaways

- Generators engage in person-centered planning to find solutions that are tailored to employees' real wellness needs.

- The person-centered planning process has three parts: provoking honest and transparent responses, suspending judgment, and showing empathy. This three-part process helps employees feel safe sharing their real wellness struggles with you and allows you to truly hear and respond to their challenges in ways that drive more effective long-term solutions.

- Generators have to invest time in person-centered planning in the beginning. But such planning saves them time in the long run, as they better understand how to flexibly and adaptably respond to varied challenges their team members face. Plus, employees themselves become empowered to suggest solutions that address the root causes of problems they are facing.

Worksheet 8.1

The Power of Person-Centered Planning

Generators practice person-centered planning as they work with team members to address their unique wellness needs. This planning process involves three core steps.

Brainstorm a few ideas on how to implement each step.

1 Provoking Honest & Transparent Responses

Brainstorm how to create a more comfortable environment for your employees to provoke honest dialogue.

2 Suspending Judgment

Reflect on times you've struggled with judging others as they share struggles and challenges. How can you change this behavior?

(Continued)

The Power of Person-Centered Planning

3 Showing Empathy

Reflect on your empathy. Is it easy for you to step into someone else's shoes? If not, how can you practice taking their perspective?

Additional notes:

Chapter 9

Eliminating Mental Health Stigma

[There's] been a really strong push [for normalizing mental health conversations] in the last few years that I've seen [in my company]. And I think a lot of people are starting to feel more comfortable and open with it. There was a campaign [about admitting you're struggling with mental health] that was launched as well, just to further emphasize that, you know, it's okay to not always be positive about things, or it's okay to not always be in a happy-go-lucky mood, and that sometimes we all struggle—and that's a part of the human condition. So that's been really heartwarming for me personally. But then to also hear from other people who have gone through challenges from a mental health and mental illness perspective, [who are] finding the right resources and being on a path toward wellness has been just incredibly enriching for me to experience and to witness."

—Melanie, telecommunications leader, study participant

To kick this chapter off, we want to take a moment to acknowledge all that you have learned about becoming a Generator thus far. In Part I of the book, you learned how to be authentic and vulnerable with your team. You got comfortable with showing them that you're a real person and learned valuable tips for showing others who you really are at work. In Part II of this book, you learned how to lead by example, set the right tone, and become a confidant to your team

175

members. Without you sending clear, consistent signals to shape your team's work environment, team members will struggle to truly care for and support their own or others' well-being. In Part III, you learned how to be flexible and become a boundary bouncer. Keeping and setting boundaries is tough, but it's important. You learned from Generators how they did so, and now you can put those practices into place yourself. In Part IV, we put these concepts together to help you master a strategic process that ensures you meet the individual needs of your team members—person-centered planning. You've learned so much already, so congratulate yourself for getting to this point.

We have one final important lesson about how to be a Generator that brings together a number of the concepts you've already learned. In Part V, the final section of this book, we detail the challenges that you may face as a Generator and help you finalize an action plan for putting the strategies you learned in place. But, before we do that, we are going to focus on this final pillar of Generator behavior: how to eliminate mental health stigma on your teams.

Before we talk about the how-tos of eliminating mental health stigma at work, what do the terms "mental health" and "stigma" mean? The World Health Organization defines *mental health* as "a state of mental well-being that enables people to cope with the stresses of life, realize their abilities, learn well and work well, and contribute to their community."[1] A *mental health disorder* occurs when there is an absence of mental well-being, such that people are unable to cope with life's stresses, face challenges in participating fully in daily life, and struggle to recognize their potential.

Finally, *stigma* occurs when others make judgments about a person or group, using labels and stereotypes to define them, in ways that result in their being outcast, devalued, or discriminated against.[2] Especially in cutthroat, traditional workplaces, where any sign of weakness can be misconstrued as a fatal flaw, talking about mental health struggles, or asking for help when they arise, can be taboo. Often people with power have the most influence over who is stigmatized and who is not. Like bullies on the playground, when someone in charge wants to cast others in a negative light, they are likely to gain greater support for their views because they are in a leadership position. But there is good news.

Leaders can have outsized influence on destigmatizing others as well. So, the power is in your hands as a leader: You can choose to encourage others to look down on stigmatized team members, or you can help your team to understand their perspective and avoid stereotyping or judging them. Generators do the latter. They deeply understand the importance of supporting employee mental health. If you help combat the stigma that those struggling to maintain their mental health often endure, you will be better able to show that you support all of your employees, even during tough times.

Mental Health Problems Are Common

Although talking about mental health struggles, such as anxiety or depression, may still be taboo, such struggles are extremely commonplace. In fact, according to the World Health Organization, one in eight people globally live with a mental health disorder.[3] That's roughly the same number of people who get the flu annually. Odds are very high that you or someone you know has experienced a mental health issue. If you don't know anyone who has, it's more likely that they just haven't told you about it.

Mental Health Stigma Is Real

Despite the frequency of these experiences, stigma around mental health continues to exist. Can you imagine what it would be like if the flu was stigmatized in this way? Imagine if employees with the flu tried to hide it and just continued working as normal. That sounds miserable—both for them, because they'd have to continue working when they really need to rest and recover, and for you, because you'd be sacrificing their work quality by pushing them to ignore their struggles. As we've learned before, this behavior backfires in the end when employees ultimately burn out. Especially since the COVID-19 pandemic, if someone incurs a physical illness, they are often encouraged to stay home and rest. Many employees, even if remote, log off and take time to recover from physical ailments. Overall, it's much more normative to discuss physical health issues and for leaders to recognize that ill employees will not be as productive as when they're at peak health.

Contrast that with how many workplaces treat mental health. Some employees experience more chronic conditions that require adjustments to their daily ways of working, if possible and within reason. In more severe situations, they may need to take a medical leave to care for their mental health, which they should do if necessary. But in many, less severe cases, employees will simply have harder days and easier days. Today, most people suffer through the harder days without sharing their struggles with others. Instead, they come to work but hide how they feel. What if, instead, those employees were able to take a day or two to try to feel better? Or if they were supported in leveraging a solution that helped to alleviate some of their struggles in the moment? Logically, that approach makes way more sense. When people feel forced to ignore their struggles, issues that are keeping them from working effectively remain unresolved and can snowball into larger, more serious challenges. If people with the flu forced themselves to work full days, they would likely stay sick longer and be less productive for a lengthier period. Instead, if they rest and recover, they can come back to work sooner and be more productive and effective when they do. Although taking a couple of days away from work may not eliminate a mental health challenge, it can help alleviate some of the negative side effects that employees experience, bringing them back to a more stable state and having an impact similar to resting when you have a physical illness.

> The more information and exposure people have to others' mental health challenges and disorders, the more stigma is eliminated. Exposure opens employees' eyes to the idea that people like them struggle with mental health—and it helps put a human face to a label or stereotype.

Having open discussions about mental health challenges and solutions may also help to surface reasonable adjustments that can be made to the ways in which employees work when struggling with mental health. These solutions might help employees cope with challenges better on an ongoing basis, eliminating the need for short-term bouts of time off.

Mental Health Stigma Hurts Employees

Why is mental health so hard for leaders and employees to discuss? It's because mental health stigma is very real. Although society has slowly grown more accepting of conversations about mental health, and these slow changes were further accelerated by the COVID-19 pandemic (a physical health challenge that had severe mental health consequences for many), the stigma around it persists. Don't think you stigmatize people with mental health challenges? You might want to examine that assumption a little bit closer. In fact, in a 2021 study, researchers found that a majority of managers were hesitant to hire someone with a mental health issue, even though they were in work environments and a broader cultural context that reflected mental health inclusion.[4] In other words, saying that you are accepting of people who struggle with mental health challenges may sound nice—or make you feel better about yourself—but, even if you're in a context that has good policies and practices when it comes to mental health, it doesn't mean that your or others' attitudes have changed. People often make work-related decisions that are rooted in deep-seated stigmas that are hard to shake. Unfortunately, the fear that employees with mental health struggles have less potential to succeed is still prevalent.

It's a theme we heard in our study as well. Participants told us about experiences with Extinguishers who either didn't support their mental health or actively stigmatized their mental health problems. Unfortunately, not only do Extinguishers propagate harm through their continued stigmatization of mental health, but they also create a work culture where employees fear the impact of disclosing their mental health challenges. Indeed, people often believe that talking about their mental health in the workplace might prevent them from being hired or promoted, might result in unfair treatment or gossip, or might make them feel left out or ostracized at work.[5]

For example, Daria, the HR analyst you met in Chapter 3, discussed her experience with mental health stigma, saying:

> On the negative side of things, I've also had managers who, if you say anything about mental health, there is such a strong stigma about it. Sometimes it puts a bigger burden back on the associate where they say things like "Well, are you able to continue your work?" Or they're not supportive. They make it more about "What is the loss impact of you having whatever mental health issue that you're going through right now? What is the impact on me and my business for that?"

As Daria recounted, when Extinguishers heard that employees were struggling (if employees even felt comfortable revealing that information), they immediately made it about them and the business, instead of seeing things from the employees' perspective. This approach makes employees feel expendable, and it instills in them a sense that their struggles are viewed as a bother instead of useful information that can help create more realistic plans for unlocking their full potential. It is also nonstrategic. When an employee is struggling, and you force them to ignore their struggles or make it clear that your only concern is the here-and-now for the business, you lose the opportunity to build support systems that might help alleviate some of their struggles in the longer term.

How Generators Support Mental Health

Like many of the wellness topics we've discussed thus far, many leaders have a hard time recognizing that supporting mental health is actually beneficial for the business and its profitability. Instead, they focus on the short term: how a small loss in productivity can impact their goals today. Leaders, and businesses in general, tend to be very shortsighted. Yet, if they zoomed out to see the big picture, they would realize that supporting mental health today promotes long-term benefits for the company, such as retention, loyalty, commitment, and engagement. Generators take this longer-term view and support employees who face mental health challenges. But in doing so Generators face a unique challenge themselves. Not only do they have to help reduce others' stigmatizing attitudes about mental health on their teams, but they need to work on gaining the trust of employees, to assure them that disclosing mental health challenges will not lead to negative outcomes. Generators may have to deprogram employees who have had to hide their mental health challenges from leaders before they feel comfortable sharing their struggles.

Generators Actively Reduce Stigma

It should be clear by now that Generators lead in a way that ensures that everyone thrives—including those who face mental health challenges. Reducing stigma toward those who struggle to maintain their mental health also helps to boost other Generator behaviors. For example, it encourages authenticity and vulnerability and, as we've discussed, it's a very person-centered way to support your team members. Regardless of their personal experiences with mental health, Generators understand that each employee's experience can be very different from their own and from each other. Thus, they actively focus on destigmatizing mental health problems to make it more likely that issues and challenges that team members are grappling with come to the forefront. They also ensure that those who share their struggles feel broadly supported in doing so (both before and after disclosing). Generators need to show that they aren't judgmental of those with mental health challenges, instill that same attitude in others, and show real allyship to those who reveal their struggles. Specifically, in our research, we found that Generators focus on three key things when eliminating mental health stigma:

1. Showing vulnerability and sharing their own mental health struggle statements, when appropriate

2. Using inclusive language when discussing mental health (e.g., using names of diagnoses, like obsessive-compulsive disorder, only when discussing a formal diagnosis; avoiding the word "crazy" to describe colleagues, etc.)

3. Using educational interventions (e.g., workshops, keynotes, trainings) to help themselves and others understand mental health challenges more deeply

Generators Have Mental Health Struggle Statements

We learned in Chapter 3 that when leaders are vulnerable, employees feel like it's okay to be vulnerable too. Generators know that normalizing vulnerability starts with themselves. Sharing your struggle statements that you created in Chapter 3 is a great first step in setting the stage for further vulnerability. But because mental health issues are so stigmatized, we give special consideration to writing a struggle statement related to mental health here. (See Worksheet 9.1 at the end of the chapter.)

Although it may be tough to do, we encourage you to draft a struggle statement related to mental health as you continue your Generator journey. Most people have experienced setbacks that have challenged their ability to stay happy, healthy, and focused. You may have experienced something diagnosable, such as anxiety, depression, or posttraumatic stress disorder. Or you may not have been diagnosed but have experienced some similar feelings or symptoms—times of extreme despair, or worry, or fear. The point is not to equate your experiences to those of others (e.g., comparing your short stint of sadness after a loss with an employee's chronic depression) but rather to show that you recognize people may not always be mentally at their best, and that's part of the human experience.

These struggle statements are probably not the first thing you should share as you begin to be more vulnerable with your team. But even though you might wait to share your statements, you should have them prepared and ready. In most instances, instead of diving right into your mental health stories, you should work toward sharing them when you've gained the trust of your team. Keep them handy, though, as you may need these struggle statements sooner than you think. You never know when the opportunity to relay them to others might arise. As you build vulnerability on your team, someone may come forward with their mental health challenge before you share your own. Be ready to share your stories to create camaraderie and trust—helping the employee feel even more supported as you do what you can to help them. Remember not to equate your story and experience to theirs. The point isn't to show that you have gone through what they have gone through or understand exactly how they're feeling. Simply use your story to show that you are open to the dialogue and understand that mental health struggles are real. This might also encourage them to share their challenge in more detail. Use the worksheet at the end of the chapter to begin drafting your mental health struggle statements. Take time to get it right, and perhaps run it by some family members or friends for feedback.

- Do your statements convey your own vulnerabilities to mental health struggles?

- Do they exclude sentiments that might be viewed as insensitive (i.e., trying to say that you have experienced the same exact thing, if you haven't)?

- Do they include clear statements of support and care?

All these components will help strengthen your mental health struggle statements.

Now let's go back to Melanie and how she was able to share her mental health struggles. We shared her story and the tragic loss of her brother in Chapters 2 and 3. Vulnerability became particularly important for her as she coped with grief and the subsequent challenges that came her way. As you'll recall, she became a stronger leader as she continued to open up and share her difficult experiences instead of keeping them to herself. As she followed the example of her own leaders and became more comfortable being vulnerable, she began to recognize the need to take things a step further. She needed to talk about her mental health.

Melanie now recognized the power in being honest with her team, something she would have never done in the days before she discussed her family tragedy. Not only did she share what had happened, she also told her team about the impact that it had on her mental health. When asked about the outcomes of doing so, Melanie said:

> Being able to tell other people my own personal journey from a mental health perspective [helped with] getting some help and support in times of need and dispelling the myth that, you know, mental health or mental illness is weakness. [I was] really encouraging people to care for themselves in that way.

We love Melanie's story. She showed a willingness to change, which amounted to massive growth as she worked toward becoming a Generator. She continued to push back on norms that were keeping employees from being their true selves and worked hard to make the work environment safer and more supportive for everyone. Melanie was able to learn from the actions of the Generators before her and to implement her own effective practices for helping her team. We know sharing personal and vulnerable details can be hard. But, as Melanie mentioned, the hardest part is getting started. As you share more of yourself, these disclosures become easier and more natural over time, even when discussing stigmatized topics. As Melanie expanded her vulnerability into the realm of mental health, it became okay for her team to do the same. She noted these powerful ripple effects that her actions had, sharing that her employees began to tell their stories and seek advice from her and others when needing support. She said:

So, for instance, when there would be a big event happening in society and that could trigger some sort of emotional reaction, there were some resources that I would get ahead of time [and share]. Like for the election for instance, that was one thing that [I said]—"Hey, this can be a really difficult period of time."

Generators not only lead by example but also work to ensure that their team members don't feel ashamed, or like burdens, for sharing their mental health challenges. Luckily, Daria, the HR analyst, had positive experiences in addition to the negative ones we shared earlier. She discussed how she was able to share her struggles openly with Generators, ask for the resources she needed, and get them—no questions asked. This support helped her feel like her leaders were being truthful when they opened the doors for her to be more vulnerable about her issues, without consequence. She said:

I've definitely been in the place where I've had to request time off to go to counseling or see therapists or things like that. And I've had managers who are really supportive. When you are clear about that or you're open or vulnerable and you say "Hey, I need to take time off for X, Y, and Z reasons," they're very supportive. And they're like "We're super-flexible. Feel free to integrate that into your month's or your week's [schedule]"...I say that's always been really, really successful when there's just no questions asked. If you say "Hey, I need to take time off for a mental health reason," they just pick up, say "That's fine," and they're very supportive.

Melanie and Daria both saw the benefits of being vulnerable in discussing mental health. Melanie saw ripple effects that helped others feel comfortable and confident in sharing their struggles. Seeing that her leaders practiced what they preached made Daria feel comfortable and valued as she disclosed her mental health issues. Both of these conversations helped destigmatize the topic more broadly and allowed Melanie and Daria both to get and to give necessary support.

Generators Know that Language Matters

In addition to actively sharing their mental health experiences, Generators are careful with the language they use when they talk about mental health. Because language can shape people's beliefs and ideas, avoiding problematic language can help reduce stigma toward those with mental health struggles, and may even make it more likely that they will seek help or treatment for issues they face.[6] In turn, employees with mental health problems will feel less excluded or "othered," and other employees' perspectives on mental health may undergo a shift. Generators can signal their values and beliefs about mental health by carefully and strategically choosing their words.

Shifting your language may seem like an easy fix, but doing so is quite challenging. Commonplace words and phrases are so embedded in our vernacular that we don't even notice when we're saying them. For this reason, it is hard to stop using certain terms. But progress is important. Doing your best and correcting yourself when you catch your own mistakes is helpful, and shows positive intentionality.

Also, being open about the fact that you are trying to stop using certain words or phrases can be impactful. Ask your team to correct you if they catch you. Doing so will cause them to think twice before using those words themselves. It'll help lead to a cultural shift that's more inclusive and sensitive to mental health struggles.

So, what does intentional language around mental health look like? First, Generators are careful when using clinical terms. Likely

Eliminating Mental Health Stigma

you've heard people using specific diagnoses to describe their behaviors or feelings. Have you ever heard someone who is compelled to be extremely organized call themselves OCD (i.e., obsessive compulsive)? Or have you heard someone say they're so "depressed" because a sports team they love lost the championship game? Both of these individuals may act or feel in ways that seem similar to the symptoms of certain mental health disorders, but they don't actually have the disorders. Why is the inaccurate use of diagnostic terms a problem? Insensitive language can minimize the experience of these mental health disorders and send a signal to employees with those disorders that colleagues don't understand what they are dealing with, which can be very harmful. Making light of such disorders can cause people to doubt their own experience and diagnosis and make it harder for them to be vulnerable and share their stories.

Second, Generators also avoid using words like "crazy" or "insane" when describing people and situations. Although it's not ideal to use words to disparage people or situations, there may be times when you are looking for an alternative. Consider using words like "wild" or "absurd" instead. Overall, using inaccurate or disparaging language can create a less safe space for people managing mental health disorders and can promote broader, more stereotypical thinking about them. Generators are aware of this and do their best to avoid this type of language. Even more important, they stop others from using that language when they hear it.

Take a moment to reflect on the language related to mental health you use at work. Use Worksheet 9.1 to brainstorm alternative words and phrases to replace terms you commonly use. Plus, consider ways you can influence others to use more accurate and inclusive language. Remember that no one is perfect and making this switch can be challenging. But slow changes over time can add up. Can you decrease your use of problematic words by some percentage? Can you commit to having compassionate conversations with employees who may be unwittingly promoting a stigmatizing environment for those with mental health challenges? Don't let trying to be perfect get in the way of progress.

Interventions at Work Can Help

Finally, Generators understand the importance of education in helping reduce mental health stigma. Research backs them up. Studies have found that training employees about the importance of mental health, and the mental health challenges that their colleagues may face, can increase positive attitudes about mental health struggles and decrease stigma toward them.[7] In addition, these interventions have been found to boost employee awareness about the impacts of maintaining positive mental health at work, improve in-depth knowledge about the mental health challenges others may experience, and increase supportive attitudes and behaviors toward those struggling with mental health.[8] As a Generator, you don't have to be the foremost expert in mental health. But you can locate people who are and bring them into your workplace to share their expertise. Being open and willing to provide and promote these resources will show your team that you value dialogues about mental health and that you are also willing to continue to learn and grow. In other words, although you may not have all the answers, finding those who do and helping others to learn from them can go a long way toward destigmatizing mental health issues.

For this reason, Generators encourage learning and programming to help educate employees on mental health. Jaya, a program manager, shared how helpful this was for her and her team:

> For one of the events [we] got some people from [a mental health resource nonprofit] here for psychological resources, and they were talking about how easy it is as a staff member to tap into these resources. . .I attended this workshop and I was like "Oh my God!" So I got involved. Oftentimes

it's [i.e., mental health challenges] also stigmatized within my [ethnic group]. God forbid you go and see a psychologist, because then your label is "crazy." But having it kind of endorsed by the leadership—it was really helpful. So I was like "It's normal. It's okay [that I have these challenges]." And then I, as a leader, can't promote the psychological resources unless I've experienced them. I don't feel comfortable doing that ever to anybody. So I was like "Okay, I have to go to this to see how to experience it, so that I have a story to tell."

Jaya's leaders allowed her to feel more comfortable sharing her own story by providing training that supported meaningful dialogue about mental health. The message they sent by organizing this important educational session helped her move past the stigma she experienced with her own challenges and to try something new to care for herself. It also ultimately led her to practice good behavior with her team and to share her story with others as she grew her own leadership capabilities. Jaya also seemed more comfortable sharing this story, knowing that her team members had also attended this training.

Let's go back to Melanie again. She made it part of her mission as a leader to destigmatize mental health after seeing the power of doing so, through all of her personal challenges. She also provided further resources for her team to deepen everyone's knowledge about the topic. She told us:

To really show people who have gone through a mental health journey and what that's been like for them, and how they've been able to leverage the resources [we provide], I was able to host a panel of folks [about decreasing mental health stigma], which was great.

Melanie intuitively knew what the research supports. Remember, the more information and exposure people have to others' mental health challenges, the more stigma is eliminated. Attending these trainings and workshops opens employees' eyes to the idea that people like them struggle with mental health—and it helps put a human face to a label or stereotype. It's harder to feel negative about people once you've really listened to them and learned more about their story. In the same way, Melanie was able to bring her own experiences forward, as well as stories from others across the company, to open an impactful conversation. As a result, her team began revealing their own mental health challenges and finding ways to support each other.

As a Generator, we recommend that you focus on vulnerably sharing your mental health journey when appropriate, using inclusive language in regard to mental health, and facilitating educational interventions to help members of your organization (and yourself) understand mental health more deeply.

Key Takeaways

- Mental health problems are extremely common, with one in eight people globally living with mental health disorders.

- Stigma toward those struggling with mental health continues to exist within organizations and our broader society.

- Generators fight mental health stigma by being vulnerable about their own mental health challenges.

- Generators also speak inclusively about mental health, avoiding words like "crazy", especially when describing others at work.

- Generators take it upon themselves to help educate others within their teams to understand mental health more deeply.

Eliminating Mental Health Stigma

Mental Health Struggle Statement

Think about your mental health journey. What have you struggled with in the past? Is there something you are struggling with today? Do you have close family or friends who have had struggles? Write three mental health struggle statements to help you relate to others.

Try these as starting points:

1) "I struggle with _____ ."
2) "I find it harder than most to _____ ."
3) "I haven't found a way to overcome _____ ."
4) "I used to have a hard time with _____ ."
5) "Early in my career, I couldn't figure out how to _____ ."

_____
_____
_____
_____
_____
_____
_____
_____
_____
_____
_____
_____
_____
_____
_____
_____
_____
_____
_____

Eliminating Mental Health Stigma

Language Matters

The words we use matter. They can contribute to continued stigmatization of mental health issues or help in eliminating the stigma. Consider how you can adjust your language to be more inclusive.

Think about the words you currently use in your daily language. Do you say things are "crazy"? Have you used mental health diagnoses to describe your quirks?

Take a moment to reflect on what words you want to stop saying.

Possible Alternative Words

Wild   Absurd

Sad

Nervous   Ludicrous   Unhappy

Apprehensive

Ridiculous

Concerned   Worried   Meticulous

Jot down the words you want to use to replace those problematic words in your daily language.

Part V

Final Thoughts and Actions

The final part of this book addresses inevitable challenges you may face on your journey toward becoming a Generator. First, you learn how to anticipate and plan for roadblocks that you may encounter on your path to generating wellness. Then, in Chapter 11, we summarize the key takeaways from the book and provide you with an action planning toolkit. This toolkit will help you map out your short-term and long-term goals and the steps needed to achieve them.

Chapter 10

Challenges and Backlash

I think sometimes you don't really know what's going on in other layers of the organization. So I know [my Generator], when she was a direct manager and she was reporting into a director, I felt like her rules and the way that she operated was much more stringent versus when she became a director herself and had a lot more leeway in giving her managers the ability to lead their teams in the way that they needed to. And then also for her to say "Sure, work from home for two days. You don't have to be in the office." So I did notice that sometimes senior leadership and the person that your manager is reporting to has a big impact on what others are feeling, you know, rippling through the organization.

—Izzy, recruiting manager, study participant

By this point, you've learned almost all the steps to becoming a Generator. We've given you clear, actionable ways that you can start to become the leader you want to be, right away. So, we hope that you have lots of ideas about how you can kick off your journey. Plus, we help you to action plan in even more detail in the last chapter. For now, though, take a moment to reflect. How are you feeling? Excited? Motivated? Nervous? Scared? The journey toward becoming a Generator may not always be easy. It's normal to have some questions, hesitations, or fears come up as you read this book. Before you start action planning, we want to make sure that we help you anticipate roadblocks that might be in your way.

Thus, in this chapter, we outline the core challenges that Generators might face during their journeys. Instead of hiding from these challenges, or using them as an excuse not to become a Generator, we hope that you can plan for them and navigate them effectively. It's important to know what problems you might encounter on your journey to prevent them from holding you back from fulfilling your potential. First, we are going to outline some challenges that you might face along the way to becoming a Generator. But don't worry! We don't leave you with a laundry list of problems. We also provide possible, effective solutions. Finally, at the end of the chapter, we show you some strategies for managing and recovering from stress that may occur as you encounter and tackle challenges.

Combating Cultures of Overwork

There is one challenge Generators face that we hear about over and over again—overwork. What happens when your team doesn't have enough time or people to do the work? What if your executive team is all about building a "lean" organization (otherwise known as an understaffed, overworked organization)? As we have discussed throughout this book, overwork is problematic. It can have negative implications for health, wellness, and productivity. Unfortunately, it's a reality many of us face. We heard numerous stories about Generators who tried to combat cultures of overwork by making subcultures for their employees within broader, more negative work environments. We know this can be challenging to do. When your boss and other coworkers believe that time equals productivity and don't believe that employees can work smarter, not harder, you can be seen as an outcast in the workplace.

That's what happened to Rashida's leader. Rashida's small, boutique consulting firm had a culture of overwork that her Generator tried to overcome. But the problem was challenging to tackle. Rashida shared:

> Being a small organization and having a dominant culture of "You work harder, and you put in the hours, and you show that you'll do whatever you need to do to succeed" was something that came up regularly with annual [performance reviews] and associates. And that's what they were seeing rewarded for the most part. It's actually one of the dominant reasons that I left and became an independent consultant. Even though [my prior manager] was creating somewhat of a safe bubble, he couldn't really create a completely safe bubble within the context of the organization as a whole.

Sometimes there's only so much you can do. But Rashida did sing praises of this Generator who worked hard to create a safe zone for his team. The dominant culture is hard to beat, but you can make things easier for folks overall.

In another example, Luna, a lead growth and sales employee, discussed how her Generator was combating a work environment focused on overwork and onsite time. At the tech startup she worked for, senior leaders were pressuring her manager to make the team show up early to the office. They wanted to see the hours that were being put in—even when it didn't make the most sense for the team's productivity. She recounted:

> But it was a culture where everybody is flocking in at 8:00 am, regardless of whether you're a senior leader, regardless of whether you're a line worker. And [my manager's

boss] definitely went and mentioned to my manager, on more than one occasion, "What is up with Luna? There are people looking for her at 8:00 am and she's not there." My manager definitely defended me in all of those instances and said, "Well, she's available if you want to just text her or call her." Because, I mean, I *had* been working since 8:00 am. I just wanted to avoid the rush hour because I lived an hour away from the site. So there were those instances where my manager would come and tell me that this is happening. [She would say,] "There's other leaders who are sort of expressing concerns over when you're coming in. But I am trying to sort of make the case that this isn't just one individual's behavior. It's the beginning of a movement that we need to go on culturally in terms of workplace flexibility. And because, if we're trying to transform, this is one of the elements of that." So, yeah, it was definitely not a smooth ride. But I always had the buy-in of my manager and, ultimately, I think the results were also speaking for themselves. It wasn't like she was defending [me] for nothing. Everything that we needed to deliver on in terms of projects and initiatives were all going great. It's just that there was no reason to be obsessed with facetime.

Luna's leader understood the importance of flexibility for Luna's particular situation. Had the leader fallen in line with what the senior leadership wanted, Luna's days would have become much longer and her risk of burnout from overwork would have increased. Luna spoke highly of her Generator and appreciated the extra effort put in to fight back against a negative culture.

Now let's go back to Ada, the business partner we met in Chapters 5 and 6 who had a great, flexible Generator. Her Generator faced pushback when trying to get her the appropriate amount of leave after the birth of her second child. Ada shared that she wanted to take an additional month of unpaid leave after her second child. (She had been able to do so with her first.) In between her two pregnancies, though, the company merged with a larger organization. This new company did not allow that type of leave and was denying her request. Her company wanted to make an example of her for precedent. Her leader ultimately prevailed, and Ada got to spend one more important month with her newborn baby. Her Generator stepped in to push back against the chief human resources officer:

> The issue got escalated up to our chief human resources officer. Actually, at the time, we moved to a discretionary paid time off [PTO] model. I didn't even have a PTO bank that I could be like "Okay. Well, I'm applying this," you know? After a big, dramatic to-do about it, my boss was like "Okay. Well, you're telling me that, as a manager, I can't grant unpaid time. But I do have the authority to grant discretionary PTO. So, I'm going to give her PTO." So I [actually] got the time paid.

Ada's leader stepped in, got creative, and got more than what was asked. Her leader did not give in to an inflexible policy and took a risk by granting PTO. It paid off for his relationship with Ada. She was loyal and committed to him and worked hard in helping him achieve his goals. Rashida, Luna, and Ada all had strong leaders who fought back against cultures of overwork and inflexibility. They stepped up and made a difference in their employees' lives.

Cultures of Overwork Are Toxic

Nobody wins in a culture of overwork. Unsurprisingly, leaders like you can get burned out in these environments too. But leaders' burnout may be particularly potent because it can trickle down to employees.[1]

That means when you're burned out, your team members will inadvertently be impacted and become more burned out too. When your burnout has ripple effects, it's particularly important to attack burnout at the root. In many organizations, the root cause of burnout is an organizational culture that glorifies overwork, rewards unhealthy work behaviors, and punishes employees who have an appropriate work-life balance. How do you combat these cultures?

Luna's leader was able to push back directly on her boss, but doing that may not be a real possibility for some Generators. We want you to have a long career and to get as many great work opportunities as possible. While we don't want you to overblow risks and stay silent for no reason, circumstances can limit Generators' ability to be effective in the long term. For example, some bosses will take out their frustrations on Generators. If you don't navigate the situation carefully, there could be real consequences associated with angering such leaders (e.g., not being promoted, being demoted, or being intimidated or harassed). If this situation is like yours, we have three suggestions:

1. Focus on the vital few.
2. Keep track of metrics.
3. Find champions.

Next we dig deeper into each of these possible solutions in your battle against overwork.

Focus on the Vital Few

The first, and possibly most important, skill to hone if you are battling a culture of overwork is prioritization (with a splash of negotiation). We encourage focusing on the *vital few*—the most critical and impactful priorities that are absolutely necessary for business success. If you can get your leaders to focus on output and results of the vital few priorities, you'll be in a better position to influence those leaders.

What if you are at the top with no leader above you? Congratulations! You don't need to ask permission to prioritize. Your job is to set realistic priorities for the teams that report to you. Check in with them to deeply understand the amount of effort and time the priorities you set require. Will your list of "the vital few" allow them to maintain a healthy workload? Always add at least 10% to the time and resource estimates for your goals. Ensuring that everyone is at full capacity for the entire year is probably too much. You need some wiggle room. Refocus on what are truly the vital few or add more people to the team.

Think about the way your leadership team sets expectations today. How involved are you in setting those expectations? Can you get more involved? Your leaders may be cascading priorities and goals to your team, but it's important to understand exactly what those priorities and goals are. In other words, it's important to know what priorities and goals your leaders consider to be the vital few. First, ask your leader to have multiple conversations around the goals and priorities so you can fully understand them. This approach can help buy you time to digest the priorities, gather information, and provide input as needed. In your first conversation, start by asking questions about why certain goals are important. What's the broader organizational impact they are trying to make? How will these goals impact the bottom line? How are they related to broader organizational goals or peer team goals? Understanding the full context of each priority will help you determine what really matters to your senior leadership and what goals may merely be nice to have.

Once you have that initial conversation, identify how long certain tasks may take. Involve your team and get their input on levels of effort and timelines. Get a sense for their current capacity and ongoing tasks to know what their workload looks like. As you map out your team's time and capacity to achieve the goals and priorities being set, make sure to add a cushion for emergencies, vacation, sick time, and development opportunities (training, conferences, etc.). Use all this information in your next conversation with senior leaders on goals and priorities. If you have an Extinguisher as a leader, it's okay to fib a little and add that cushion of time to your overall estimates (without revealing that you've added it).

Consider building a spreadsheet to map your priorities, timelines, and capacity across the team. This spreadsheet can show your senior leaders that you are prepared and taking your leaders' goals seriously. As you look at the team's capacity, if you see gaps where capacity will not cover what needs to be done, create an argument for more resources or a narrowing of priorities. The goal is to be very planful with your leader and demonstrate that you are aligned and onboard with meeting objectives. Most leaders like to think they are good at planning so they may appreciate your approach and be open to discussion. Once it's clear that you want to achieve their goals, they may take you more seriously when you flag resources that you'll need, suggest adjustments to timelines, or recommend making changes to the status quo. If you show you're on their side, they might be more likely to be on yours.

What happens if your leader won't budge at all on priorities? If they don't agree with the capacity as you laid it out? Unfortunately, that happens. Generators understand they aren't close enough to the work to always know how long things take. Extinguishers, in contrast, assume they know it all.

If you are faced with a situation like this, we recommend you email your concerns so you have documentation that the team may not meet certain current timelines without more resources. You can say the team will try to be on time, but do not make any promises. You can use email as cover if deadlines are missed. Identify the biggest pain points for the team and keep bringing it up in one-to-ones with your leader as you approach those challenging times. In those conversations, have the data and insights to back up your concerns to avoid appearing as if you are just programmed to say no. (In those one-to-ones, don't forget to highlight the team's good progress and wins, such as other projects and deadlines that are on target.) As the deadlines get closer, your leader may become more flexible out of fear of how missing a deadline will look for them. Ultimately, if your team can't make the deadline, your leader will look ineffective to their more senior leaders. As deadlines approach, some Extinguishers will communicate softer deadlines to their leaders or throw additional resources at the problem to avoid looking bad. You can capitalize on that tendency.

Unfortunately, even with good planning and negotiation with your leader, things rarely go as planned. The plan is really more of a tool to help you to keep the dialogue on priorities going. Never ask for permission to prioritize. Make it clear that mapping out priorities is a must for your team. Inevitably, the priorities your leader sets will change. They may ask you for something new or ask you to prioritize an existing goal more urgently. When that happens, tell your leader you need to reprioritize your team's workload. Use the spreadsheet you already built and map out what this change may do to the team's capacity. Let the leader know that something will have to be deprioritized or delayed to make room for a new ask. Sometimes that's enough for the leader to change their mind about asking.

If not, spend time negotiating deadlines for already ongoing priorities, push back on timelines, and be vocal about what is possible in the time allotted.

Even Generators who are fantastic at prioritizing can fail with an Extinguisher above them. Focusing on the vital few priorities your leader truly cares about can be effective if you're working with leaders who are willing to have some discussion. But if you are dealing with a dictator, consider the next two possible solutions to help you tackle a culture of overwork.

Keep Track of Metrics

Another possible solution to combating cultures of overwork is to use data to prove your point. Data can help you show why it's important to support employee wellness. This tactic is particularly helpful when you are dealing with leaders who assume their gut instincts are always right.

First, start by pulling data from external sources—like this book or other publications, reports, and studies—to back up what you are arguing for. If you can figure out what sources your executive team or senior leaders like, look at those to help support your arguments. Odds are that any source they are reading may have some data on why employee wellness matters. Once you've pulled those resources, consider how you can track metrics yourself. Does your organization have an employee experience survey? Can you see your team's data and how it compares to the broader organization? If senior leaders are tracking engagement, job satisfaction, and intent to stay with the company, you may already have some of the data you need to tell the story. If you only track these metrics annually, consider taking initiative to ask these survey questions to your team midyear as well, to gather more data to support your arguments. You don't need a formal process to do that—you can collect the data yourself, using an anonymous survey sent just to your team.

What if your organization doesn't track metrics on employee health and wellness? That doesn't mean you can't track them yourself. Just as you can create a subculture on your team, you can also create your own practice for tracking metrics associated with the positive changes you are making on your Generator journey. In other words, if you're going to spend a lot of time focused on being a Generator, you can make the most of your efforts by measuring the impacts. Doing this might sound intimidating, but a couple of survey questions can reliably capture employee attitudes.

Developing Your Survey

Not sure what survey questions to ask? Luckily, Google can be your friend. Look for Employee Experience (EX) Survey Vendors, and you may find a few sample questions to use. You don't need many.

A solid survey approach is to provide statements (like the following examples) and have employees rate how much they agree with the statement (strongly disagree to strongly agree):

1. I am satisfied with my job.
2. I would recommend the company as a great place to work.
3. My direct leader manages priorities effectively.
4. My workload is manageable.

The first two questions are likely linked to increased performance and productivity. The second two questions can give you some insight on whether you are managing overwork effectively. These are great starting points in showing that more positive attitudes and reasonable workloads can lead to better outcomes.

When it comes to measuring outcomes, you may already be tracking employee performance, but likely only once a year or so. This timing may not be frequent enough to assess changes associated with your Generator practices. Consider documenting employee performance on a more regular basis. You can track some ratings on your own or consider getting qualitative feedback from external stakeholders on the performance of your team. Don't ask for anything formal from clients or customers. But, in quick conversations, collect some thoughts about how your team is doing. That way you can show it's not simply your assessment of performance that matters. Also keep track of other results. Think about on-time project completion, customer satisfaction scores, or any other key performance indicators that may be relevant to your team (and that you may already have access to). Objective data can help you tell a richer story to naysayers about the culture you are creating.

How do you use all this data? You don't need to do anything complicated. You can simply look at trends. If you can show that the average level of satisfaction and performance improved on your team after implementing some changes on your Generator journey, you may have a much easier time showing people why these changes matter. If you recall, Luna's leader was able to do this, and it had positive effects on her leader's ability to sell her hunch that having more facetime with employees did not always boost their performance.

Not a data scientist? That's okay. Using data to tell a story can be fairly straightforward. We recommend starting with a spreadsheet that simply tracks your numbers. What's your average employee engagement score? What's your average performance score? What percentage of projects hit their deadline? You can track this data at whatever frequency you collect it and see if the numbers improve over time. Or you can get fancy and make a line graph showing the trend. There's no need to overcomplicate. Simple statistics can make your point.

Note that data collection may be difficult sometimes. Employees may be hesitant to answer survey questions if they know you can see the answers. This is true even with Generators who are highly trusted. It's hard for employees to be open with their feelings about their jobs and their companies if their responses can be traced back to them. Never force employees to identify themselves. If you are simply looking at trend lines, anonymous responses are okay (and maybe even more honest). Also, you may want to refrain from gathering data if you have a very small team. Spotting changes on a small team may be harder than on larger teams. Plus, even anonymous surveys are identifiable if only a couple of people are responding.

If you can't use a data-driven approach, there's one more solution to try when battling against overwork cultures.

Find Champions

If prioritization isn't working and you can't easily use metrics to make your case, we recommend finding champions who can support you in your fight against overwork. Most organizations we studied have at least one or two Generators who truly understand the importance of employee wellness. Do you know who those people are in your organization? Ask yourself these questions to identify those Generators:

- Whom do people love to work for?
- Who has a great reputation for being a leader who takes care of their people?
- Whose team has the highest retention rate?

If you are struggling to gain support for your Generator behaviors, try to engage with these champions. Finding a champion may be especially important for demographically underrepresented leaders, like women and racial minorities, whose actions may be overly scrutinized compared to their peers. In this instance, finding a champion from a majority group (e.g., men or White leaders) may be particularly useful for amplifying your message. While our data showed that Generators came from a variety of demographic backgrounds, this approach may be useful if your organization has traditionally lacked representation in the leadership ranks.

First, set up a conversation to explain the challenges you are facing. An honest dialogue between two like-minded people can go a long way. Ask if they might be willing to help you strategize about how to gain support for your Generator journey. Alternatively, ask if they are willing to join you in spreading the word about the importance of these behaviors in your organization. Perhaps you could even organize a panel or workshop to discuss these issues together more broadly. Consider making this conversation a recurring one. Building a relationship with a fellow Generator can help you feel less alone on the journey. Plus, you can both benefit from a new, meaningful friendship at work.

As Pippa, a manager of learning at an aerospace company, shared, it is critical to have buy-in from someone at the top. Champions can serve in that role even if they aren't in your direct reporting line. She said:

> I think the biggest thing would be having that buy-in from the top, having leaders at the top of the organization that support wellness in a holistic way. So, kind of building that culture and helping us feel like you can take a vacation and that's okay. You can go to your son's soccer game and that's okay, without getting side-eye from anyone. I don't

know if you'll ever do away with [cultures of overwork] entirely but that would be kind of my ideal. I think that some buy-in at the top is a great [starting point].

Although having someone more senior as a champion is amazing, it's also important to recognize that all champions may not hold formal leadership roles. Lower-level employees who have influence over others can also help. Imagine the power of partnering with folks on your team to present about the positive impacts that Generator leadership has had on them and their work. Sometimes hearing from influential employees who have benefited from Generators can help others see the importance of addressing negative, overwork cultures.

Keeping Extinguishers at Bay

Generators don't face challenges only from the top and the broader culture. Often they are roadblocked or sidelined by Extinguishers on their team. While you may technically lead the team, employees with negative attitudes can bring down those people you are trying to lift up. Extinguishers are not just bad leaders. They can be anyone who sucks the energy and positivity out of an otherwise happy and well-functioning team. They can be truly detrimental to the efforts of even the best Generators.

Jaya, the program manager we met in the last chapter, shared that certain members of her team often created an environment that ran counter to what her Generator was trying to instill. She said it had negative impacts on her well-being and ability to function at her best. She recounted:

> We were welcoming students back for a party. . .so the rest of the staff is all white. I was talking to them while

we were checking in students and one of the alumni came over and [he] was saying that he moved from Puerto Rico. [My coworker] started to say that if he moved from Puerto Rico, he had to hop a fence to get here. And [my other coworkers] all laughed and they all repeated it to each other. As a Latina, I shouldn't have to explain how painful that is to hear.

In other words, despite your best intentions, others' energy and behaviors matter. Sometimes being a Generator is not enough to turn around the attitude of every single person you interact with or who reports to you. Luckily, we have suggestions for overcoming this barrier.

One way to combat Extinguishers on your team is to use the power of group norms. In Chapter 4, we talked a lot about setting the right tone. As you enact Generator behaviors, your team culture will be strengthened. And, as this occurs, team members will start to keep each other in check when someone deviates from team norms that support employee wellness. As we discussed, this makes your job easier. You don't always have to be around to call out the behaviors that detract from this norm.

But in addition to setting that tone, you can make it more likely that team members will promote and encourage positive behaviors from each other in a couple more ways. First, work to create closeness on the team itself. Bring the team together to engage in social activities and fun team-building activities. A close-knit team cultivates stronger norms but also feels more comfortable engaging in tough conversations with one another. The more you can create connections between team members, the easier it will be for them to come to a consensus on their culture—and to hold each other accountable to it.

Second, you can recognize and publicly acknowledge Generator behaviors that you see in your team members. In doing so, you will be providing positive reinforcement for those behaviors. When people see leaders reward something, they will respond positively to those same types of behaviors. It's harder for Extinguishers to continue with their negative behaviors if they know that others will view them poorly for it. Plus, if they see that the opposite behaviors are being rewarded, they may start to align so they can reap the same rewards. If you are dealing with the trickier situation of an Extinguisher who is actively trying to undermine colleagues' Generator behaviors, your positive reinforcement will make those trying to be more like Generators feel appreciated and empowered, which might help them to continue on the positive path they are on.

When you build a strong team that has a positive and cohesive culture, members are more likely to maintain and take care of that culture in the long term. Cultivate this type of work environment by giving your team dedicated time and opportunities to get to know each other better, uniting them with common goals, and clearly letting them know what behaviors are valued and expected. These types of cultures make it harder for Extinguishers to persist.

Sometimes a Generator, Sometimes an Extinguisher?

When we first started talking about the results of our research with organizational leaders, they posed an interesting question. What if an employee is only an Extinguisher sometimes but at other times is neutral or even a Generator? How do you handle an inconsistent, less predictable Extinguisher?

Let's think of some examples. Imagine an employee who is absolutely wonderful and supportive in dealing with clients and senior leaders but who is more negative and less encouraging toward peers or those more junior to them. Or imagine a moody employee who can be a wonderful contributor to the team culture one day and, on another day, can be rude and dismissive of their peers. Or think of an employee who is willing to step in and help when workloads get high or someone has a family issue to attend to but gets judgmental and resentful when someone takes a vacation longer than a week.

This situation is different from grappling with an employee who is more consistently an Extinguisher. Dealing with inconsistent Extinguishers can be confusing, and, unfortunately, it may be easier to let them off the hook for their "bad moments." If they behaved poorly yesterday but are doing well today, you may not want to discourage them while they are doing well. Yet it's important to find ways to improve their Extinguisher behaviors, even if they aren't always displaying them.

Luckily, with a "sometimes Generator, sometimes Extinguisher," there is a glimmer of hope. This employee does the right thing some of the time. Consider how you approach the person to reinforce those good behaviors. Can you document the good things they are doing? Maybe you can give them immediate positive feedback when they are acting like a Generator. Now consider the times they are exhibiting Extinguisher behaviors. What types of situations provoke these behaviors? Is it a stress reaction or related to mental health?

We encourage you to have honest one-on-one conversations with the inconsistent Extinguisher. Spend time talking about all the great things they do to contribute to the positive culture you are cultivating. Be honest about your own Generator journey and how excited you are to see others on the team exhibit these types of behaviors. Then mention that at times they deviate from these positive behaviors. Provide an example and ask them about it. Why did they react negatively to someone taking a long vacation? Seek to understand root causes of their behaviors, and partner with the inconsistent Extinguisher to become a more consistent Generator.

It's possible that these negative behaviors stem from mental health issues or personal situations that are impacting inconsistent Extinguishers. Consider ways to help support employees to get them to a better place mentally, allowing them to manage their reactions and responses more effectively.

Understanding the root cause can help you know how to resolve the problem. If the behaviors are not due to a serious underlying personal or mental health concern and you have the resources, consider investing in coaching or a leadership development program for inconsistent Extinguishers. It may be just the nudge they need to become full-time Generators.

If these employees do well some of the time, they probably have some level of good intent behind their behaviors. Capitalize on that by telling them you see their potential if they improve in some key areas or address the underlying problem. Then provide them with the support and resources to do so; they might surprise you.

You Can't Please Everyone All the Time

Unfortunately, you can't always win the battle against Extinguishers and bad cultures. As a Generator, it's important to recognize a simple but difficult fact: You can't please everyone all the time. While it is worthwhile to try to be the best leader you can be, there may be naysayers or those who are unhappy with your efforts. The important thing is getting it right most of the time. You aren't perfect—no one is—and that's okay.

Sometimes Generators have to learn to cope with the challenges of being trailblazers. It can be a hard road at times. Zara, an HR leader at a food company, shared that her leader was more than willing to take a stand on tough issues and recognized that Generators sometimes have to be agitators to make change. She told us:

> She is very much someone who doesn't really care about what people think of her or what she's doing. So, she doesn't mind pushing back on things, which is very helpful

to have as a manager. Because she will be the person to raise her hand and say, "I don't agree with this and here are all the reasons why." So, it's been nice to have someone who supports me in that way as well.

Generators can handle criticism, pushback, and the displeasure of others. If you are in an environment where not everyone is aligned with the Generator approach, you may have to get comfortable with some tension.

As a Generator, you are flexible and supportive of the individual needs of your team members. But what happens when team members' needs conflict with each other? Let's say you have an employee who wants to return to the office and interact with the team face to face. But other team members are completely disinterested in spending time in the office. How do you handle a situation where employees have discrepant needs and you want to tailor your approach to them all?

We have a solution that enables you to deal with stubborn naysayers and to craft solutions that meet employees' discrepant needs.

Ultimately, communication is key in situations where you can't please everyone. You may not be able to win over naysayers, but you can ensure that you consistently share the power of your approach in a compelling way. Although naysayers can be roadblocks at times, they serve as a useful mechanism for gaining respect from others. Naysayers give you an opportunity to demonstrate that you are willing to stand up for your beliefs and for your team members, even when doing so is hard. If you calmly and consistently communicate your case for being a Generator, you can show others that you are willing to stand by your principles in the face of adversity.

Communication is also important in instances when you are unable to meet the needs of employees because they clash with others' preferences. Sometimes it's impossible to please all parties, as in the example of facetime versus remote work. If you can't meet an employee's needs, have an honest conversation about your intentions to help support them while explaining why it may not happen for this one request. Also, consider compromises. Maybe it's impossible to have daily face-to-face interactions with colleagues, but you could consider having monthly in-person meetings as a team. It's a small ask of employees who get the flexibility to work from home to help build positive relationships with other employees with different preferences.

Remember Monica, the data analyst at a large retailer? She mentioned that her prior leader—whom she considered an Extinguisher—disappointed her because she rejected her request to be relocated without explanation. Monica stated that it would have been much better if the leader had at least explained why her request couldn't be honored or if the leader had shown earnest consideration for her needs. Instead, the leader rejected Monica's request outright, which was more frustrating to Monica than the decision itself. When you have to make a tough call, being intentional about setting aside time to debrief the employee who is being impacted can help. It shows you care enough about the employee and their request to give it the time it deserves.

Sometimes these open conversations can lead to important brainstorming on how to address the problem or the request differently. Maybe the employee who wants to return to the office will share that they are really seeking more opportunities to get to know their teammates individually. That can lead to brainstorming ways to encourage coffee chats across the team—even if virtual—where people can have some of those casual, bond-building conversations. Or perhaps the employee will share that they just struggle to work from home and thought pushing for a return to the office could help them to be more efficient. As a solution, perhaps you could provide funds to help them access a coworking space a few times a month.

Challenges and Backlash

Working with employees directly to come up with creative solutions to their challenges and needs is part of what Generators do. Having meaningful conversations when you aren't sure how to support an employee can help to jump-start that process.

With all the possible challenges along your journey, from cultures of overwork to inconsistent Extinguishers, we encourage you to prepare for these roadblocks. Use Worksheet 10.1 at the end of the chapter to help you brainstorm what challenges you anticipate and how you may overcome them.

When All Else Fails, Recover

We've talked a lot about how to overcome challenges as you journey toward becoming a Generator. However, these challenges may take time to defeat. And you may lose some of your battles. A severe overwork culture may not change. Prioritizing your own well-being is okay too. Dealing with these challenges can be stressful and could add to what you already have on your plate as an effective leader. So, while we are big proponents of top-down or more systemic solutions, we recognize that some strategies to improve your own wellness may be useful on your journey.

One particularly impactful way to improve your wellness is to recover after work. A plethora of research can help guide your efforts in after-work recovery. Bonus: You can share all these tips with your team to help them recover outside of work as well.

The four key ways to recover after work are relaxation, detachment, control, and mastery.[2]

1. For *relaxation*, you might just need to chill out by watching TV, lying around and doing nothing at all, taking a bubble bath, or listening to music. Perhaps you already recover after work in these ways. Many people lean into relaxation when

they are feeling particularly exhausted after a long workday. Although relaxation isn't the most effective strategy for recovery, it does work to some extent. We don't recommend engaging in this strategy exclusively, but you should definitely feel free to relax when you want to.

2. *Detachment* is a second way to recover. Detachment is all about fully disconnecting from work. And that means house and family chores as well. Completely ditch your technology when you detach. Get out in nature—away from your computer, email, or other "pings"—or spend time with friends and family (minus screens). When you truly disconnect, you have time to recover from the constant pressure of being "on." You can just be. Research has also shown that detaching after work can help you to feel less exhausted and more energetic while you're at home.[3] So when you detach, not only can you feel better at the end of the day, but you'll be a better contributor to your family, friends, and household too.

3. *Control* is the third way to recover. This approach may seem a little odd. But doing things that make you feel in control can help you recover from a long day at work. When we are in control, we feel a greater sense of autonomy over our work and our life. We like to feel that we have control over our destiny, instead of being thrown down a path that isn't our own. To gain control, take some time to actively plan your week or the month ahead. In addition, setting boundaries and keeping them is another form of control. So, if you plan to go for a hike on Friday but you need to stop working an hour early to do so, you can practice both detachment and control.

4. *Mastery* is an extremely effective recovery strategy. Mastery entails getting better at something you really like to do and that's not work-related. One of the reasons that mastery is so

effective is because working toward something that is tough, but enjoyable, is beneficial to us as human beings.[4] If you love art, take time to paint. If you love martial arts, set a goal to get a new belt. Into cooking? Make some recipes you haven't tried before. The list goes on and on. As we progress through our careers, we often forget about hobbies that once made us very happy. What are those hobbies for you? Picking one or two of them back up can be a great way to recover from work-related stress.

Consider your own preferences when you work toward recovery. If one of these strategies stands out as the most effective for you, that may be the one that most improves your well-being.[5] Your recovery is meant to help you. These research-based tactics are a great place to start thinking through what types of recovery you want to try. Experiment with these strategies and figure out what combination helps you recover the most. As you think through your preferences and try new strategies, use Worksheet 10.1 to reflect on and find what works for you.

Further, recovery strategies can be taught. Research shows that managers who are trained on how to recover tend to have lower stress, better sleep, and more positive emotions when compared to managers who are not trained.[6] If you don't feel like you understand recovery tactics that well, you might want to engage in more in-depth training to develop your recovery skills. For example, you might have a hard time understanding how to detach from work. Consider seeking out courses that can help you learn how to effectively detach, possibly using tools like mindfulness. Research shows that this type of training works.

Ultimately, as you traverse the windy road to becoming a Generator, dodging roadblocks and battling challenges head on, make sure you are taking time to manage your own stress and recovery. An unwell Generator can't stay a Generator for long. You'll burn out and become unable to help others. Help yourself first and practice good recovery.

Key Takeaways

- Cultures of overwork can get in Generators' ways. But focusing on the vital few, keeping track of metrics on your own team, and finding champions can help you defeat these cultures.

- Extinguishers can serve as roadblocks for Generators. Building team cultures of camaraderie and offering training and support to Extinguishers who show glimmers of promise can help.

- Remember that you can't please everyone all the time. But consistently communicating your intentions can set the stage for meaningful conversations that might result in greater respect from others and better solutions for addressing the challenges employees face.

- If ongoing stress is getting you down, use recovery tactics to keep yourself afloat until more structural, systemic changes to your work environment are possible.

Worksheet 10.1

Challenges and Backlash

Reflect on what you just read in the chapter. What challenges do you think you will face? How can you handle them? Use the space below to brainstorm ways to approach the roadblocks you may face.

What challenges might you face? (Think culture of overwork, Extinguishers, etc.)
List each potential challenge.
For each potential challenge, brainstorm two possible solutions or ways to approach it.

Challenges and Backlash

Recovery

Now consider the recovery tactics outlined in the chapter. Take a moment to brainstorm recovery tactics that you can use to combat the stressors on your journey to becoming a Generator.

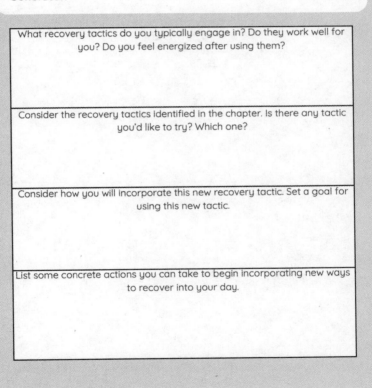

What recovery tactics do you typically engage in? Do they work well for you? Do you feel energized after using them?

Consider the recovery tactics identified in the chapter. Is there any tactic you'd like to try? Which one?

Consider how you will incorporate this new recovery tactic. Set a goal for using this new tactic.

List some concrete actions you can take to begin incorporating new ways to recover into your day.

Chapter 11

Action Planning

Working for [Greg] for [nearly 20 years] did a lot to shape how I am as a leader. And I model the behaviors I saw from him in terms of working with my own direct reports. I now have two people from my old team who are in management roles themselves and they've taken the lessons they learned from me, that I learned from [Greg], and they're using them in terms of how they interact with their own employees.

—Liam, analytics manager, study participant

First. . .you've reached the last chapter of the book. Congratulations! You've learned everything you need to know to create the workplace you have been striving for. You've learned that Generators have a huge impact on their employees—making them happier, healthier, and more productive. They also have a lasting impact on employees, often building future generations of Generators. More than that, you've learned all the tools you need to become an effective Generator. Now it's your turn to put your learning into action. You've done a number of reflections and activities preparing you for this moment. We hope that you feel excited and energized to start taking steps to become a Generator.

What You've Learned

Before we dive into your action planning, let's do a quick recap of what you've learned. We hope you keep coming back to this chapter anytime you need a refresher. Also revisit Worksheet 11.1 at the end of this chapter as frequently as needed to keep on track with your action plan.

Why Workplace Wellness Matters

In Chapter 1, you learned why workplace wellness matters. When leaders support employee wellness, employees are healthier, perform better, achieve their goals, and are more committed to their work. In addition, when employees feel better, they are also more committed to the supportive leaders and team members who helped them to feel that way. In turn, they help leaders achieve their goals, band together with others to tackle challenges, and ultimately create more innovative and productive workplaces. For these reasons, improving employee wellness can also boost organizational profitability and have a broader, positive impact on society. Happy, healthy employees bring positivity to their communities, making the world a better place.

No One Wants a Superhero

In Part I, you learned that employees don't want superheroes for leaders. We talked about firing your work self and embracing your struggle statement. As we described, employees want authenticity from their leaders. In other words, they are looking for leaders who show their true selves at work. They do not trust inauthentic leaders who seem to put on a façade when they come to work. Employees trust authentic leaders because they believe these leaders are more willing to be transparent and honest, no matter the situation. Employees can then better predict how their leaders will behave.

This predictability makes employees more likely to take risks by sharing their own truth and by raising important issues that good leaders would want to have on their radar. As a result, employees with authentic leaders perform better, are more productive, are more engaged, and have better well-being.

But being authentic doesn't have to always be about sharing deep secrets about yourself. Generators often start small by sharing little details about themselves, such as their hobbies and interests. You can do the same. If sharing your authentic self seems intimidating, choose something that seems pretty easy to reveal and work your way up to bigger challenges. To practice these skills, you also wrote your first struggle statements. *Struggle statements* are simply tools to help you communicate a set of challenges or difficulties you face at work, both past and present. When you are open about your struggles, employees can build their trust in you, and your openness helps them open up to you. This situation is great for employees and for leaders because teams that can be open about their struggles usually do so because they are in a safe and supportive environment, which also makes them more productive and higher performing.

Do you know why you haven't always been authentic at work? Understanding the reasons can help you on your journey to becoming a Generator. Take a moment to reflect. How authentic are you really? What stops you from being authentic?

It's the Tone, Not the Time

In Part II, you learned that it's the tone that Generators set, not the time they spend working, that matters. You learned about setting the right tone on your team and how to become a confidant swiftly. Being a role model for balancing work and life, along with showing positivity and gratitude toward your team members, can help inspire employees to follow your example. As we discussed, positivity and gratitude are both contagious. When leaders share these sentiments with their employees, those employees start to spread the same positivity to others. Employees are motivated to help each other out if they see you and other team members doing the same. Generators create cultures of work-life balance, positivity, gratitude, and helping. These cultures save them time, as team members themselves begin to practice good behaviors.

Further, Generators understand how to become confidants to their employees quickly and meaningfully by leveraging the *SWIFT process*. As you learned, SWIFT includes:

- Setting aside time specifically for building relationships (and, remember, more time is needed at the beginning of a new relationship)
- Welcoming others warmly
- Intentionally inquiring about employees' lives
- Following up with appropriate questions to dig deeper
- Taking time to reflect on how to improve relationships with employees

One more important step is key: Once you've built the relationship, it's crucial to maintain it. If you can follow the SWIFT process and maintain those deep relationships over time, you'll be able to create a long-lasting, thriving team environment very quickly.

Work Should Support Life

In Part III, you learned that work should support life, instead of the other way around. You learned that it's important to be elastic—to demonstrate flexibility and recognize that your way isn't right for everyone. You also learned the important skills of protecting and respecting your employees' boundaries between work and life. Generators are *boundary bouncers*—they help employees set boundaries, serve to enforce those boundaries, and block employees from people or situations that violate their boundaries. Boundary bouncers also protect their own boundaries, leading by example.

Generators value work-life balance and also recognize that employees' preferences for how to balance their work and lives may be different from their own (and from other employees'). You learned that preferring segmentation rather than integration is a primary way in which employees differ in how they want to manage their work and lives. Segmenters like to keep work and life separate, while Integrators like to merge the two domains. You also gained an understanding of how to create work environments that better match employees' unique needs and preferences in managing their work and life. Supporting employees' boundaries and work-life balance is crucial for achieving shared team goals. When Generators earn employees' trust, make employees feel cared for, and act in ways that honor employees' preferences and needs for managing work and life, they retain their employees longer.

One Size Doesn't Fit All

Then, in Part IV, you learned that one size doesn't fit all when it comes to wellness. You learned about *person-centered planning* and how to use that process for your employees' benefit. Engaging in person-centered planning can help you find solutions that are tailored to employees' real wellness needs. This process has three parts:

1. Provoking honest and transparent responses

2. Suspending judgment

3. Showing empathy

This three-part process helps employees feel safe when sharing their real wellness struggles with you, and it allows you to truly hear and respond to their challenges in ways that will drive more effective long-term solutions. You have to invest time in person-centered planning in the beginning. But doing so saves you time in the long run as you better understand how to flexibly respond to varied challenges your team members face. Plus, once you start engaging in person-centered planning, employees become empowered to suggest solutions that address root causes of problems they are facing.

Further, you learned that even though mental health challenges are common, stigma toward those struggling with mental health problems continues to exist within organizations. Generators fight mental health stigma by being vulnerable about their own mental health challenges. To get you started on that path, you created a *mental health struggle statement*. Generators also speak inclusively about mental health—like avoiding calling others "crazy." Plus, Generators use experts to help their teams understand mental health more deeply. By engaging in person-centered planning and eliminating mental health stigma, you can learn about what employees really need and want at work, while helping them also gain true acceptance and validation from others.

Challenges and Backlash

Finally, in Chapter 10, you learned about challenges, backlash, and how to recover from the stressors you may face on your journey. Cultures of overwork can get in your way. But focusing on the vital few, keeping track of metrics on your own team, and finding champions can help you defeat these cultures. Extinguishers can also serve as roadblocks for Generators. Building team cultures of camaraderie and offering training and support to Extinguishers who show even small glimmers of promise can help.

Remember that you can't please everyone all the time. Consistently communicating your intentions can set the stage for meaningful conversations that might result in greater respect from others and better solutions for addressing the real challenges employees face. And, as a last resort, if ongoing stress is getting you down, you can use the four recovery tactics—relaxation, detachment, control, and mastery—to keep yourself afloat. Sometimes using those tactics is key for Generators to sustain themselves along their journeys, until more structural, systemic changes to their work environments are possible.

> If you're unwell, you can't stay a Generator for long. You'll burn out and be unable to help others. Help yourself first and practice good recovery.

How to Build an Effective Action Plan

Now that we've recapped all you've learned, it's time for you to build your action plan. We are huge fans of action planning because it turns good intentions into positive behaviors. You'll never be as motivated to put what you've learned into action as you are right now. The best way to ensure that you become a Generator is to turn your motivation into a clear action plan as soon as possible.

To do so, first take a moment to reflect on all that you've learned. Where do you think your biggest opportunity areas are? In the first iteration of your action plan, you'll want to focus on a couple of larger areas of opportunity that you are currently lacking skills in and one secondary area of opportunity that you have some skills in but can strengthen and refine. Use Worksheet 11.1 at the end of the chapter throughout this section. We'll guide you through what to do.

Know Your "Why"

To start, take a moment and revisit your "why." Why are you interested in becoming a Generator? What drove you to pick up this book? What kind of leadership legacy do you want to leave behind?

Jot down your "why" before you start your action plan. (See Worksheet 11.1.) It'll be an important reminder as you journey toward becoming a Generator. If you stumble or run into major challenges, you can always revisit and recenter on your "why" to help drive you forward.

Set Your Goals

Next, you will want to define three goals for your journey. Now that you've completed the book, you may have more than three goals in mind. But working toward too many things at once can be overwhelming—and it makes you less likely to achieve your goals. We suggest starting with three initial goals and then setting more goals after you've achieved those. Remember that every small step you take toward becoming a Generator will help you. The bonus is that many of these behaviors build on each other. It's also important to keep in mind that developing your skills truly is a journey. It'll take time to shift your behaviors, but it's well worth it. As you identify your three goals, here are a few things to consider:

- *Think about the order of your goals.* Start with the concepts at the beginning of the book first. They build on each other in important ways. For example, you can't expect employees to share their specific needs with you during your person-centered planning if you haven't created a safe, vulnerable, and authentic relationship with them first.

- *As you think through the contents of this book, figure out which of the chapters (in order) you need the most help with.* Maybe you are vulnerable and authentic with your team, but you set a bad example for work-life balance. Since you can check concepts 1 and 2 off the list, start with how you set the tone on your team as your first goal.

- *Then consider the difficulty of addressing the areas of opportunity you are identifying.* Setting the right tone is going to take more time than writing a struggle statement, for example. Also, think about setting goals in the same area that is hard or new for you, instead of crafting all three goals across different areas of opportunity. For example, maybe you need to work at setting a better example of work-life balance. You might set two meaningful goals around role modeling work-life balance to tackle this area of opportunity more comprehensively. If your first two goals seem very challenging, think of something a little easier for your third goal. If you are not overwhelmed, you build momentum toward achieving your goals. If you're already a pro at showing vulnerability with your team, perhaps your third goal might be to simply write down three new struggle statements, so you are a little bit more prepared to be vulnerable in the future.

Did you figure out what your goals are? If so, it's time to start refining them. When defining your goals, remember to make them SMART (**s**pecific, **m**easurable, **a**chievable, **r**elevant, and **t**ime-bound):

- *SMART goals are specific.* You want to be very clear on what each goal is. Your goal shouldn't be "I want to be a Generator," for example. Although that may be your ultimate goal, it's not specific enough for action planning. For example, if your goal is to be more vulnerable or authentic with your team, a more specific SMART goal might be that you want to share three new

233

Action Planning

things about yourself with your team in the next three months. Not only is that specific, but you can *measure this goal* (the M in SMART). Over time, you can keep track of how many new things about yourself you share with your team.

- *You also want the goals to be achievable and relevant.* Using the example of sharing three new things about yourself with your team, you can see that this goal isn't too lofty and unrealistic. It's very reasonable to think you can share a few new things with your team. This goal is also relevant because doing so is clearly tied to what you are trying to achieve: being more vulnerable and authentic at work.

- *Finally, you want your goals to be time-bound.* In other words, you need a deadline. In the example goal, we made a timeline—to share three things in three months. If you leave the goal too open, you are more likely to push it off and not achieve it. By keeping yourself accountable to a timeline, you will find greater success in sticking to your goals.

Gather Necessary Resources

After setting your goals, consider what resources you may need along this journey. Would an accountability partner help? If so, find a peer leader to share your goals with and ask them to keep you accountable to achieving them. Ask this person to check in with you a couple of times a month to see how you're doing.

Or maybe you need a mentor instead of an accountability partner. If you think you need more guidance on how to implement these behaviors, consider finding a Generator you know or have heard about in your organization. Ask them to mentor you and guide you through this journey. Can't find a mentor? Consider investing in a coach. If you have the funds from work (or personally), some coaching to help support you on your journey may be beneficial.

Are there other resources that you need to help you along your journey? Maybe you are already at maximum capacity and don't have time at work to accomplish much of anything outside of your job duties. Consider fighting for more headcount to help alleviate your time constraints. More staff will free up time for your own self-development. Or simply talk to your leader. Explain why investing in your development as a Generator can help the team and its goals.

Continue to think through the ways you will achieve these goals and any other resources you may need. You can also come back to this section after you've gone deeper into the details of your goals.

Get Detailed with Your Goals

Now that you've completed the first page of Worksheet 11.1, the next three pages are dedicated to your three chosen goals. Dedicate one page to each goal. First, spend some time getting into the details of each of your goals. Start with why you are tackling that specific goal. Let's go back to the example of setting the right tone. Maybe you chose that goal because you tend to disrespect your own work-life balance. If so, perhaps your "why" driving that shift is because you want your team to feel okay to manage their own work and lives in a more balanced way.

After determining your "why," think about the metrics associated with achieving that goal. Remember, your goals should be measurable and time-bound. How will you know you succeeded? What can you measure that will help you know you've hit the mark? What types of concrete changes do you expect to see on the team? Make a plan to measure the outcomes you expect to achieve by making these changes.

Next, identify key dates. When will you start working toward this goal (hint: today)? When do you expect to complete the goal?

Then set some milestone dates. If you plan to share three new things about yourself in three months, maybe you expect to have shared one of those things in the first month. Write down key check-in dates to keep yourself accountable and keep track of your progress.

Now your planning gets a little tougher. But the next sections are critical to your success. As we talked about in Chapter 10, challenges are inevitable. If you anticipate those challenges and ways around them, you are much more likely to persist and still achieve your goal. Write down challenges that might get in the way of achieving your goals. Going back to the example of sharing three things about yourself with your team, maybe you identify time as a challenge. For instance, maybe time constraints in your one-on-one meetings prevent you from getting to anything besides work. How can you be more efficient in those meetings or carve out time to do more sharing? Think through possible solutions to help you overcome the challenges that may come your way. Finally, write down the specific steps you need to take to achieve your goal. Breaking your goals down into baby steps will help you start to make progress quickly, which is more motivating. What's the first thing you will do? What's the second step after that? Try to be as concrete as possible to help you see the path forward to achieving your goal.

Now do this again for your other two goals. The more detailed you can get, the better. We humans are much better at achieving goals if we understand all the paths forward and have plans B, C, and D ready if we face any roadblocks.

Key Next Steps

Now that you have your action plan in place, start to take action. Set reminders on your calendar to keep you focused as you move forward. If you decide to use an accountability partner, mentor, or coach, share this plan with them. We also encourage you to talk to your team about this. Share your takeaways from this book and how you plan to work toward becoming a Generator. That level of vulnerability can help a lot with your team. And it might inspire some of them to become Generators too. They may help keep you accountable and/or be more willing to step up and share their needs when they see you are serious about becoming a great leader.

Along the way, make sure you are also taking time to celebrate your wins. It's okay to pat yourself on the back for achieving your goals. Treat yourself to that fancy coffee or long walk as a little reward. And remember to celebrate the changes you see on your team too. Are people sharing more openly with you than ever before? Thank them—and take time to thank yourself for building trust in that relationship. Becoming a Generator can be challenging at times, so don't forget to acknowledge all the good things that are happening.

After you've achieved all your goals in your plan, come back to this chapter and see what else you should work on. What's the next step? What are the next two to three goals you should set? Becoming a Generator is not a one-and-done type of developmental plan. It'll take continuous learning and growth to reach your full Generator potential. Finally, set aside time for reflection every three to six months or so. How are things going? What can you do better? What is missing? What is going really well? What feedback have you heard from your team and/or your leaders?

To close, we want to thank you for taking time to read this book. We are so proud of you and your willingness to take these important steps to becoming the amazing leader you are meant to be. We know you will shine as a Generator and make a lasting impact, for yourself and others, as you create team cultures where everyone can truly thrive.

Generator Action Plan

WHY ARE YOU ON THIS GENERATOR JOURNEY?

| GOAL #1 | GOAL #2 | GOAL #3 |

RESOURCES AND SUPPORT NEEDED

NOTES

Generator Action Plan

GOAL #1	WHY	METRICS

START DATE	CHECK-IN DATES	COMPLETION DATE

ANTICIPATED CHALLENGES	POSSIBLE SOLUTIONS

ACTION STEPS

- _____
- _____
- _____
- _____

- _____
- _____
- _____
- _____

NOTES

(Continued)

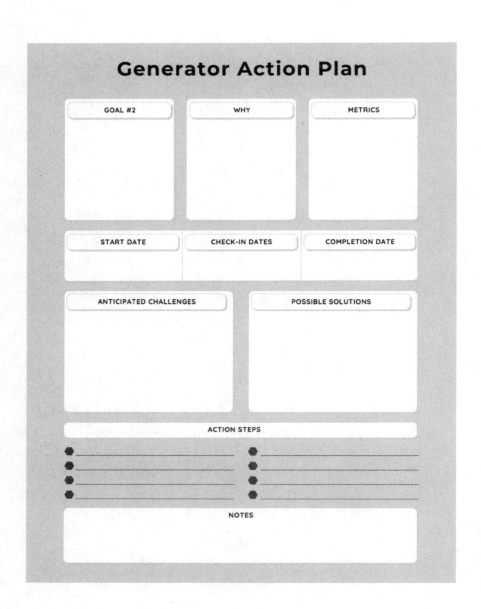

Generator Action Plan

GOAL #2	WHY	METRICS

START DATE	CHECK-IN DATES	COMPLETION DATE

ANTICIPATED CHALLENGES	POSSIBLE SOLUTIONS

ACTION STEPS

- _____
- _____
- _____
- _____

- _____
- _____
- _____
- _____

NOTES

Generator Action Plan

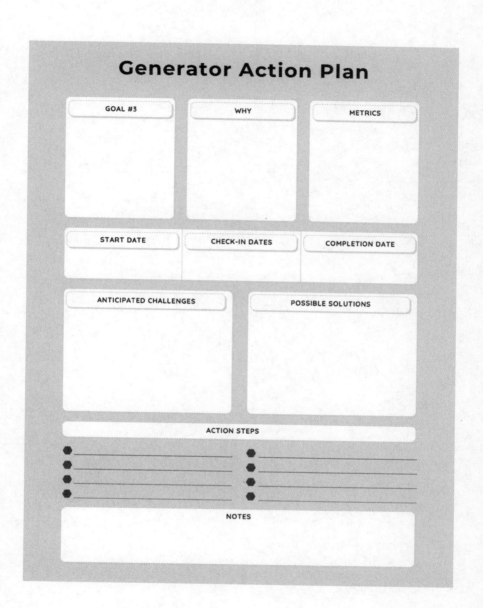

GOAL #3	WHY	METRICS

START DATE	CHECK-IN DATES	COMPLETION DATE

ANTICIPATED CHALLENGES	POSSIBLE SOLUTIONS

ACTION STEPS

NOTES

Notes

Introduction

1. Fisher, J., and Silverglate, P.H. (2022, June 22). The C-Suite's role in well-being. *Deloitte Insights.* www2.deloitte.com/us/en/insights/topics/leadership/employee-wellness-in-the-corporate-workplace.html
2. Edgerton, B., and Smith, J. (2024, January 17). "Americas board priorities 2024." *EY.* www.ey.com/en_us/board-matters/americas-board-priorities-2024
3. Grand View Research. (Accessed April 20, 2024). Corporate wellness market size & share report, 2023–2030. www.grandviewresearch.com/industry-analysis/corporate-wellness-market
4. Workhuman. (2022, October 6). "New Gallup wellbeing and workplace study finds employee recognition can help mitigate $322 billion cost of global turnover and lost productivity." [Press release.] https://press.workhuman.com/press-releases/new-gallup-wellbeing-and-workplace-study-finds-employee-recognition-can-help-mitigate-322-billion-cost-of-global-turnover-and-lost-productivity/

Chapter 1

1. Judge, T.A., Thoresen, C.J., Bono, J.E., and Patton, G.K. (2001). The job satisfaction–job performance relationship: A qualitative and quantitative review. *Psychological Bulletin 127* (3): 376–407.
2. Bowling, N.A., Eschleman, K.J., and Wang, Q. (2010). A meta-analytic examination of the relationship between job satisfaction and subjective well-being. *Journal of Occupational and Organizational Psychology 83* (4): 915–934.

243

3. Wolpin, J., Burke, R.J., and Greenglass, E.R. (1991). Is job satisfaction an antecedent or a consequence of psychological burnout? *Human Relations 44* (2): 193–209.

4. Wright, T.A., and Cropanzano, R. (2000). Psychological well-being and job satisfaction as predictors of job performance. *Journal of Occupational Health Psychology 5* (1): 84–94.

5. Wigert, B., Agrawal, S., Barry, K., & Maese, E. (March 13, 2021). *The wellbeing-engagement paradox of 2020.* Gallup. www.gallup .com/workplace/336941/wellbeing-engagement-paradox-2020.aspx

6. Yan, Q., and Donaldson, S.I. (2023). What are the differences between flow and work engagement? A systematic review of positive intervention research. *Journal of Positive Psychology 18* (3): 449–459.

7. Schaufeli, W.B., and Bakker, A.B. (2004). Job demands, job resources, and their relationship with burnout and engagement: A multi-sample study. *Journal of Organizational Behavior 25* (3): 293–315.

8. Meyer, J.P., and Maltin, E.R. (2010). Employee commitment and well-being: A critical review, theoretical framework and research agenda. *Journal of Vocational Behavior 77* (2): 323–337.

9. Becker, T.E., Billings, R.S., Eveleth, D.M., and Gilbert, N.L. (1996). Foci and bases of employee commitment: Implications for job performance. *Academy of Management Journal 39* (2): 464–482.

10. Stanley, D.J., and Meyer, J.P. (2016). Employee commitment and performance. In: *Handbook of employee commitment*, 208–221. (Ed. John P. Meyer.) Northampton, MA: Edward Elgar.

11. Mathieu, J.E., and Zajac, D.M. (1990). A review and meta-analysis of the antecedents, correlates, and consequences of organizational commitment. *Psychological Bulletin 108* (2): 171–194.

12. Ellis, A.M., Bauer, T.N., Erdogan, B., and Truxillo, D.M. (2019). Daily perceptions of relationship quality with leaders: Implications for follower well-being. *Work & Stress 33* (2): 119–136.

13. Maertz, C.P. Jr., Griffeth, R.W., Campbell, N.S., and Allen, D.G. (2007). The effects of perceived organizational support and perceived supervisor support on employee turnover. *Journal of Organizational Behavior 28* (8): 1059–1075.

14. Sun, J., Liden, R.L., and Ouyang, L. (2019). Are servant leaders appreciated? An investigation of how relational attributions influence employee feelings of gratitude and prosocial behaviors. *Journal of Organizational Behavior 40* (5): 528–540.

15. Bernerth, B., and Hirschfeld, R.R. (2016). The subjective well-being of group leaders as explained by the quality of leader–member exchange. *Leadership Quarterly 27* (4): 697–710.

16. Acar, S., Tadik, H., Myers, D., van der Sman, C., and Uysal, R. (2021). Creativity and well-being: A meta-analysis. *Journal of Creative Behavior 55* (3): 738–751.

17. Newman, A., Donohue, R., and Eva, N. (2017). Psychological safety: A systematic review of the literature. *Human Resource Management Review 27* (3): 521–535.

18. Wright, T.A., and Cropanzano, R. (2000). Psychological well-being and job satisfaction as predictors of job performance. *Journal of Occupational Health Psychology 5* (1): 84–94.

19. Van De Voorde, K., Paauwe, J., and Van Veldhoven, M. (2012). Employee well-being and the HRM–organizational performance relationship: A review of quantitative studies. *International Journal of Management Reviews 14* (4): 391–407.

20. Nielsen, K., Nielsen, M.B., Ogbonnaya, C. et al. (2017). Workplace resources to improve both employee well-being and performance: A systematic review and meta-analysis. *Work & Stress 31* (2): 101–120.

21. Q.Ai. (2023, January 31). Corporate burnout is coming for investor profits. *Forbes.* www.forbes.com/sites/qai/2023/01/30/corporate-burnout-is-coming-for-investor-profits/?sh=342a567e7008

22. Gallup (Retrieved November 3, 2024). How to prevent employee burnout. www.gallup.com/workplace/313160/preventing-and-dealing-with-employee-burnout.aspx#:~:text=The%20long%2Dterm%20effects%20of,to%20actively%20seek%20another%20job

23. Pendell, R. (2024, April 3). Employee engagement strategies: Fixing the world's $8.8 trillion problem. *Gallup.* www.gallup.com/workplace/393497/world-trillion-workplace-problem.aspx

24. Gandi, V., and Robison, J. (2021). The "Great Resignation" is really the "Great Discontent." www.gallup.com/workplace/351545/great-resignation-really-great-discontent.aspx

25. Wein, D. (2018, August 29). Council post: win with wellness—attract and retain talent. *Forbes*. www.forbes.com/sites/forbesbusiness developmentcouncil/2018/08/27/win-with-wellness-attract-and-retain-talent/?sh=c39ac1f16480; Miller, S. (2023, December 21). Wellness programs as an employee retention tool. *Society for Human Resource Management*. www.shrm.org/topics-tools/news/benefits-compensation/wellness-programs-employee-retention-tool

26. Grzywacz, J.G., and Marks, N.F. (2000). Reconceptualizing the work-family interface: An ecological perspective on the correlates of positive and negative spillover between work and family. *Journal of Occupational Health Psychology 5* (1): 111–126.

27. Suttie, J. (2024). Does venting your feelings actually help? *Greater Good*. https://greatergood.berkeley.edu/article/item/does_venting_your_feelings_actually_help

28. National Institute for Health and Welfare. (2020, March 11). Heavy stress and lifestyle can predict how long we live. *ScienceDaily*. www.sciencedaily.com/releases/2020/03/200311100857.htm#:~:text=Being%20under%20heavy%20stress%20shortens%20their%20life%20expectancy%20by%202.8%20years.&text=These%20results%20are%20based%20on,expectancy%20of%20men%20and%20women

29. Xu, H., Bègue, L., and Bushman, B.J. (2012). Too fatigued to care: Ego depletion, guilt, and prosocial behavior. *Journal of Experimental Social Psychology 48* (5): 1183–1186.

Chapter 2

1. Dirks, K.T., and Ferrin, D.L. (2002). Trust in leadership: Meta-analytic findings and implications for research and practice. *Journal of Applied Psychology 87* (4): 611–628.

2. Kim, T., David, E.M., Chen, T., and Liang, Y. (2023). Authenticity or self-enhancement? Effects of self-presentation and authentic leadership on trust and performance. *Journal of Management 49* (3): 944–973.

3. Weischer, A.E., Weibler, J., and Petersen, M. (2013). "To thine own self be true": The effects of enactment and life storytelling on perceived leader authenticity. *Leadership Quarterly 24* (4): 477–495.

4. Legood, A., van der Werff, L., Lee, A., and Den Hartog, D. (2021). A meta-analysis of the role of trust in the leadership-performance relationship. *European Journal of Work and Organizational Psychology 30* (1): 1–22.

5. Wei, F., Li, Y., Zhang, Y., and Liu, S. (2018). The interactive effect of authentic leadership and leader competency on followers' job performance: The mediating role of work engagement. *Journal of Business Ethics* 153 (3): 763–773.

6. Gardner, W.L., Cogliser, C.C., Davis, K.M., and Dickens, M.P. (2011). Authentic leadership: A review of the literature and research agenda. *Leadership Quarterly 22* (6): 1120–1145.

7. Craig, N., and Snook, S. (2014, May). From purpose to impact. *Harvard Business Review 92* (5): 104–111.

Chapter 3

1. Mayer, R.C., Davis, J.H., and Schoorman, F.D. (1995). An integrative model of organizational trust. *Academy of Management Review 20* (3): 709–734.

2. Oc, B., Daniels, M.A., Diefendorff, J.M. et al. (2020). Humility breeds authenticity: How authentic leader humility shapes follower vulnerability and felt authenticity. *Organizational Behavior and Human Decision Processes 158*: 112–125.

3. Owens, B.P., Johnson, M.D., and Mitchell, T.R. (2013). Expressed humility in organizations: Implications for performance, teams, and leadership. *Organization Science 24* (5): 1517–1538.

4. Chandler, J.A., Johnson, N.E., Jordan, S.L., and Short, J.C. (2023). A meta-analysis of humble leadership: Reviewing individual, team, and organizational outcomes of leader humility. *Leadership Quarterly 34* (1): 101660.

5. Owens, B.P., and Hekman, D.R. (2016). How does leader humility influence team performance? Exploring the mechanisms of contagion and collective promotion focus. *Academy of Management Journal 59* (3): 1088–1111.

Chapter 4

1. Barsade, S.G., Coutifaris, C.G.V., and Pillemer, J. (2018). Emotional contagion in organizational life. *Research in Organizational Behavior 38*: 137–151.
2. Fredrickson, B.L., and Joiner, T. (2002). Positive emotions trigger upward spirals toward emotional well-being. *Psychological Science 13* (2): 172–175.
3. Barsade, S.G., Coutifaris, C.G., and Pillemer, J. (2018). Emotional contagion in organizational life. *Research in Organizational Behavior 38*: 137–151.
4. Lee, L., Tong, E.M.W., and Sim, D. (2015). The dual upward spirals of gratitude and basic psychological needs. *Motivation Science 1* (2): 87–97.
5. Chancellor, J., Margolis, S., and Lyubomirsky, S. (2018). The propagation of everyday prosociality in the workplace. *Journal of Positive Psychology 13* (3): 271–283.
6. Nook, E.C., Ong, D.C., Morelli, S.A., Mitchell, J.P., and Zaki, J. (2016). Prosocial conformity: Prosocial norms generalize across behavior and empathy. *Personality and Social Psychology Bulletin 42* (8): 1045–1062.

Chapter 5

1. Robert, L.P., Denis, A.R., and Hung, Y.C. (2009). Individual swift trust and knowledge-based trust in face-to-face and virtual team members. *Journal of Management Information Systems 26* (2): 241–279.
2. Neeley, T. (2018, January 29). How to build trust with colleagues you rarely see. *Harvard Business Review*.
3. Schilke, O. and Huang, L. (2018). Worthy of swift trust? How brief interpersonal contact affects trust accuracy. *Journal of Applied Psychology 103* (11): 1181–1197.
4. Blomqvist, K., and Cook, K.S. (2018). Swift trust: State-of-the-art and future research directions. In: *The Routledge Companion to Trust* (ed. R.H. Searle, A.I. Nienaber, and S.B. Sitkin), 29–49. London: Routledge.
5. Livne-Tarandach, R., and Jazaieri, H. (2021). Swift sense of community: Resourcing artifacts for rapid community emergence in a temporary organization. *Academy of Management Journal 64* (4): 1127–1163.

6. Galinsky, A., Pandit, V.S., Schweitzer, M., and Koo, C.Y. (October 2015). Building trust: A leader's action plan. *Wharton Executive Education.* https://executiveeducation.wharton.upenn.edu/thought-leadership/wharton-at-work/2015/10/building-trust/

7. Gerace, A., Day, A., Casey, S., and Mohr, P. (2017). "I think, you think": Understanding the importance of self-reflection to the taking of another person's perspective. *Journal of Relationships Research 8*, e9: 1–19.

Chapter 6

1. Leslie, L.M., King, E.B., and Clair, J.A. (2019). Work-life ideologies: The contextual basis and consequences of beliefs about work and life. *Academy of Management Review 44* (1): 72–98.

2. Bal, P.M., and De Lange, A.H. (2015). From flexibility human resource management to employee engagement and perceived job performance across the lifespan: A multisample study. *Journal of Occupational and Organizational Psychology 88* (1): 126–154.

3. Brower, T. (2022, May 11). How the term "work-life balance" is changing for the youngest group of workers. *Fast Company.* Retrieved November 8, 2024, from www.fastcompany.com/90749429/how-the-term-work-life-balance-is-changing-for-the-youngest-group-of-workers

4. Nippert-Eng, C.E. (1995). *Home and Work: Negotiating Boundaries Through Everyday Life.* Chicago, IL: University of Chicago Press.

5. Ashforth, B.E., Kreiner, G.E., and Fugate, M. (2000). All in a day's work: Boundaries and micro role transitions. *Academy of Management Review 25* (3): 472–491.

6. Rothbard, N.P., Phillips, K.W., and Dumas, T.L. (2005). Managing multiple roles: Work-family policies and individuals' desires for segmentation. *Organization Science 16* (3): 243–258.

7. Kossek, E.E., and Lautsch, B.A. (2012). Work–family boundary management styles in organizations: A cross-level model. *Organizational Psychology Review 2* (2): 152–171.

8. Volk, S., Lowe, K.B., and Barnes, C.M. (2023). Circadian leadership: A review and integration of chronobiology and leadership. *Journal of Organizational Behavior 44* (2): 180–201.

Chapter 7

1. Koch, A.R., and Binnewies, C. (2015). Setting a good example: Supervisors as work-life-friendly role models within the context of boundary management. *Journal of Occupational Health Psychology 20* (1): 82–92.
2. Koch, A.R., and Binnewies, C. (2015). Setting a good example: Supervisors as work-life-friendly role models within the context of boundary management. *Journal of Occupational Health Psychology 20* (1): 82–92.
3. Kreiner, G.E., Hollensbe, E.C., and Sheep, M.L. (2009). Balancing borders and bridges: Negotiating the work-home interface via boundary work tactics. *Academy of Management Journal 52* (4): 704–730.
4. Allen, T.D., Merlot, K., Lawrence, R.C., Slutsky, J., and Gray, C.E. (2021). Boundary management and work-nonwork balance while working from home. *Applied Psychology 70* (1): 60–84.
5. Wepfer, A.G., Allen, T.D., Brauchli, R., Jenny, G.J., and Bauer, G.F. (2018). Work-life boundaries and well-being: Does work-to-life integration impair well-being through lack of recovery? *Journal of Business and Psychology 33* (6): 727–740.
6. Kossek, E.E., Perrigino, M.B., and Lautsch, B.A. (2023). Work-life flexibility policies from a boundary control and implementation perspective: A review and research framework. *Journal of Management 49* (6): 2062–2108.

Chapter 8

1. Rogers, C. (2021). *Client centered therapy*. London: Hachette UK.
2. Kirschenbaum, H., and Jourdan, A. (2005). The current status of Carl Rogers and the person-centered approach. *Psychotherapy: Theory, Research, Practice, Training 42* (1): 37–51.
3. Rogers, C. (1963). The concept of the fully functioning person. *Psychotherapy: Theory, Research, and Practice 1* (1): 17–26.
4. Joseph, S. (2021). How humanistic is positive psychology? Lessons in positive psychology from Carl Rogers' person-centered approach—it's the social environment that must change. *Frontiers in Psychology 12*: 709–789.

5. Joseph, S. (2020). Why we need a more humanistic positive organizational scholarship: Carl Rogers' person-centered approach as a challenge to neoliberalism. *Humanistic Psychologist 48* (3): 271–283.

6. Rogers, C.R. (1995). *On becoming a person: A therapist's view of psychotherapy*. San Francisco, CA: HarperOne.

7. Dubord, N., Parent, C., and Parent, R. (2021). Client-centered policing: A focus on positive community contacts within Canada. In: *Enhancing Police Service Delivery: Global Perspectives and Contemporary Policy Implications* (ed. J.F. Albrecht and G. den Heyer), 143–158. Cham, Switzerland: Springer Cham.

8. Pates, J., Cowen, A.P., and Karageorghis, C.I. (2012). The effect of a client-centered approach on flow states and the performance of three elite golfers. *International Journal of Golf Science 1* (2): 113–126.

9. Zaccaro, S.J., Gilbert, J.A., Thor, K.K., and Mumford, M.D. (1991). Leadership and social intelligence: Linking social perspectiveness and behavioral flexibility to leader effectiveness. *Leadership Quarterly 2* (4): 317–342.

Chapter 9

1. World Health Organization. (2022, June 17). *Mental health*. www.who.int/news-room/fact-sheets/detail/mental-health-strengthening-our-response

2. Link, B.G., and Phelan, J.C. (2001). Conceptualizing stigma. *Annual Review of Sociology 27* (1): 363–385.

3. World Health Organization. (2022, June 8). *Mental disorders*. https://www.who.int/news-room/fact-sheets/detail/mental-disorders

4. Janssens, K.M., van Weeghel, J., Dewa, C. et al. (2021). Line managers' hiring intentions regarding people with mental health problems: A cross-sectional study on workplace stigma. *Occupational and Environmental Medicine 78* (8): 593–599.

5. Brohan, E., Henderson, C., Wheat, K. et al. (2012). Systematic review of beliefs, behaviours and influencing factors associated with disclosure of a mental health problem in the workplace. *BMC Psychiatry 12*: 1–14.

6. Volkow, N.D., Gordon, J.A., and Koob, G.F. (2021). Choosing appropriate language to reduce the stigma around mental illness and substance use disorders. *Neuropsychopharmacology* 46: 2230–2232.

7. Tóth, M.D., Ihionvien, S., Leduc, C. et al. (2023). Evidence for the effectiveness of interventions to reduce mental health related stigma in the workplace: A systematic review. *BMJ Open* 13 (2): 1–8.; Hamann, J., Mendel, R., Reichhart, T. et al. (2016). A "mental-health-at-the-workplace" educational workshop reduces managers' stigma toward depression. *Journal of Nervous and Mental Disease 204* (1): 61–63.

8. Hanisch, S.E., Twomey, C.D., Szeto, A.C. et al. (2016). The effectiveness of interventions targeting the stigma of mental illness at the workplace: A systematic review. *BMC Psychiatry 16* (1): 1–11.

Chapter 10

1. Huang, J., Wang, Y., Wu, G., and You, X. (2016). Crossover of burnout from leaders to followers: A longitudinal study. *European Journal of Work and Organizational Psychology 25* (6): 849–861.

2. Bennett, A.A., Bakker, A.B., and Field, J.G. (2018). Recovery from work-related effort: A meta-analysis. *Journal of Organizational Behavior 39* (3): 262–275.

3. Demerouti, E., Bakker, A.B., Sonnentag, S., and Fullagar, C.J. (2012). Work-related flow and energy at work and at home: A study on the role of daily recovery. *Journal of Organizational Behavior 33* (2): 276–295.

4. Bennett, A.A., et al. Recovery from work-related effort.

5. Steed, L.B., Swider, B.W., Keem, S., and Liu, J.T. (2021). Leaving work at work: A meta-analysis on employee recovery from work. *Journal of Management 47* (4): 867–897.

6. Hahn, V.C., Binnewies, C., Sonnentag, S., and Mojza, E.J. (2011). Learning how to recover from job stress: Effects of a recovery training program on recovery, recovery-related self-efficacy, and well-being. *Journal of Occupational Health Psychology 16* (2): 202.

Acknowledgments

We talk about the importance of sharing gratitude at work in this book. Now it's our turn to share. We want to take a moment to express our gratitude for the multitudes of people who have supported us and cheered us on during our book-writing journey.

Jointly, we want to thank our amazing agent, Jill Marsal, for her belief in us, her detailed feedback that allowed us to polish our ideas, and her legal prowess. We wouldn't be here without her.

Thank you to our publisher, Wiley, and our fantastic editorial team, including Cheryl and Kezia. We are grateful for their support, guidance, and patience with our obsession with feedback.

We are indebted to our incredible colleagues for supporting our book-writing journey and helping us to navigate the publishing process as first-time authors. Specifically, thank you to Steven Rogelberg and Dolly Chugh, for sharing their experience and their networks. We are so thankful for their unending willingness to help us.

Thank you to our early readers—Anne Scaduto, Jimmy Karnezis, Matt Schroyer, and Heather Dunn—for providing valuable feedback and encouragement in our writing process. Special thanks to Jill Strange for not only reading our very first draft chapter but also giving us peace of mind when we wanted more feedback later in the process. Her time and energy had a huge impact on us.

We also want to thank our wonderful study participants. Without their time and insights, this book would not have been possible. We would be remiss if we didn't extend extra gratitude to Asher, who sadly lost his battle with cancer while we were writing the book. We hope his contributions and story will change people's lives for the better.

Thank you to Caroline George, our amazing intern, who supported us during the final phases of our research. We are grateful for your hard work and positive presence.

A special thank-you to our friend Nataliya Baytalskaya, who threw an amazing wedding where Workr Beeing was born. Thanks for supplying the wine!

We also want to acknowledge our Penn State I/O family. We met at Penn State and thrived with the support of our mentors, colleagues, and lifelong friends. We are!

Individually, we would like to thank our families and friends.

Patricia's Acknowledgments

I would like to thank Mom, Dad, Martha, and Jason for your excitement and encouragement along this writing journey. You've always made me feel like I can accomplish anything. And thanks to Harper for being a constant joy! Let's hope the beach house is coming soon! I would also like to thank my in-laws, Pam, Luga, Alyssa, and Luga, for cheering me on in my endeavors. In addition, I want to acknowledge the love and support from my extended family who always believe in me and my goals. Specifically, I would like to thank Roxy, Ciocia Aldona, Wujek Jarek and Gosia for listening to my ideas and providing me invaluable feedback. To all of my dearest friends, I am forever grateful for your friendships, your laughter, and your support. Rachel, Jimmy, and Matt, I am especially grateful for how you have encouraged me throughout this book-writing process. I also want to thank my own Generator, Sudha Solayappan. Thank you for always supporting me, cheering me on, and giving me the feedback and coaching I need.

I miss those who aren't here to see this book get published. Specifically, my grandparents and Jacob and Kevin Piaskowski: I know you would have loved this moment as much as I do. I miss you.

Finally, I want to thank my amazing partner in life, Daniel, for being the best support and biggest cheerleader. You always look out for me, making sure I relax and destress. You also give me the time to work on the millions of things I have going on. I don't know how many meals I'd miss if it wasn't for your cooking and checking in on me. Thank you for taking care of our furbabies—Finn, Kona, and Ray—and for making sure that I get to have fun moments on busy days. (And bonus shout-out to those sweet furbabies and all the love they give me!)

Katina's Acknowledgments

I would like to thank Mom, Dad, Matt, and Courtney for their unwavering love, support, and guidance. Special shout-out to my mom, who instilled a love of books and reading in me from a young age. Your passion for writing rubbed off on me in a big way! I wouldn't be an author if it weren't for your love, care, and encouragement. To all my extended family—aunts, uncles, cousins—you've been there to support me throughout my life and I couldn't be more grateful for each of you. Our late nights spent laughing around the kitchen counter are the best cure for anything (even writer's block). Regarding the book itself, I would like to give special thanks to Cathy Cassidy, Barbara Mooney, Deborah McCann, Carissa Fales, Mary Cate Wampler, Lilly McCann, Maggi McCann, Eugenia Cassidy, Ange Mooney, Carrie Sawyer, Mae Ledva, and Ann Ledva for cheering me on and sharing your wisdom as we brainstormed titles, content, and covers.

Thank you to my grandparents, Jennie and Augie Salvitti and Frances and Paul Sawyer, who worked hard to lay a solid foundation for our families. I will always fondly remember reading out loud to

Grandmom Sawyer as she folded the laundry. She would have been very excited about this book (and no matter how many copies it sells, she would have told everyone it sold millions).

Thanks also to Brendan for giving me the space to write this book. When life gets busy, you remind me to take time for fun. Being with you is the most fun, and I couldn't be more grateful for all you do for me (and Donnie). To all my wonderful friends, you are the absolute best (especially the St. Basil's Panther crew, Balrog, the Hound, and the Pink Ladiez). Without you, my wellness would be severely compromised. Finally, I'd like to thank my high school English teacher, Annie Boagni, who encouraged me to share my voice with the world. Thank you. I'm glad I listened.

About the Authors

Patricia Grabarek is a cofounder of Workr Beeing. She is an industrial/organizational psychologist with a passion for and expertise in workplace wellness, diversity and inclusion, workplace culture, employee engagement, leadership development, and people analytics. She has spent her career as a practitioner, mostly working in consulting but recently taking on more internal roles, leading people analytics and talent management teams. Throughout her career, Patricia has worked with over 60 different client organizations from various industries, implementing industrial/organizational psychology solutions and research to improve wellness, diversity, retention, performance, and engagement within their organizations.

Patricia was featured on Culture Amp's list of Top 25 Emerging Culture Creators for 2024 and has been featured in media outlets, including the *L.A. Times*, *CBS News*, and CBC Radio. Patricia received her PhD and MS in Industrial/Organizational Psychology from The Pennsylvania State University and her BA in Psychology from the University of California, Los Angeles.

Katina Sawyer is a cofounder of Workr Beeing and an Associate Professor of Management and Organizations at the University of Arizona's Eller College of Management. Her areas of expertise include diversity, work-life balance, leadership, and positive workplace behaviors. Over the years, Katina has published over

50 peer-reviewed studies, book chapters, and *Harvard Business Review* articles. Her work has been cited in many public outlets, including the *Washington Post, Bloomberg Business Week, The Atlantic, Forbes,* and *The Conversation.*

She has been awarded research grants from the National Science Foundation and from the Society for Human Resource Management. In 2017, Katina received recognition as Top 40 under 40 from the *Philadelphia Business Journal.* She also has extensive experience consulting with various organizations providing data-driven solutions. Katina earned her BA in Psychology from Villanova University. She earned a dual-PhD and MS in Industrial/Organizational Psychology and Women's Studies from the Pennsylvania State University.

Index

A

Action plan, building, 231–236
Action planning, 225
Attention Deficit Hyperactivity
Disorder (ADHD),
struggles, 169
Authenticity, 226–227
achievement, 40
contagiousness, 30–32
display, 39
employee need, 28–30
leaning in, 45
learning, 175–176
plan creation, steps, 33
research support, 25–27
simplicity, 29–30
Authentic self, becoming, 22

B

Become a Boundary Bouncer worksheet, 149–150
Be Elastic: Your Way Isn't Always
Right worksheet, 128–129
Bond-building conversations,
217–218
Boundaries
importance, recognition, 142–143
respect, 147
setting, 142

Boundary bouncers, 229
becoming, 131
creativity, 140
employee enjoyment, 133–135
impact, 140–143
role, description, 132–133
self-protection, 135–138
Boundary bouncing
example, leader (impact), 136
Generator
engagement, 133
modeling, importance, 137
practice, 146–148
style, Generator adaptation,
139–145
subculture, creation, 144–145
Generators, impact, 143–145
Boundary breakers (blocking),
boundary bouncer
(impact), 132–138
Boundary-breaking culture,
subculture creation, 143
Broad-minded coping, 70
Burnout, 22, 153
increase, results survey, 64–65
outside impact, 13
ripple effect, 201–202
setup, 62
workplace wellness outcome, 1–2

C

Care (display), actions (usage), 92

Career path, consideration, 107–108

Challenges and Backlash worksheet, 222–223

Champions, discovery, 202, 209–211

Change
  factors, 125–127
  willingness, 185

Client-facing role, 137

Clients
  expectations, setting, 134
  feedback, 170
  meetings, missing, 120

Communication, importance, 216–217

Community-centered planning, police engagement, 160

Company
  policies, inflexibility, 122
  power, harnessing (societal good), 3

Confidant, 95
  groundwork, 81–82
  impact, 81, 91

Contagious positivity, research support, 69–72

Control (recovery process), 219

Conversations, engagement, 83

Coworking space, access, 217–218

Culture
  creation, 67
  instruction, 61
  leaders, actions (impact), 65–68

D

Destigmatization, leaders (influence), 177

Detachment (recovery process), 219

Dialogue
  engagement, 162
  honesty, 210

Disenchantment, workplace wellness outcome, 1–2

Draft Your Struggle Statements, 56

E

Educational interventions, usage, 182

Elasticity, 107
  benefits, 123–127

Eliminating Mental Health Stigma, 192–193

Email, disconnection (effectiveness), 63

Embrace Your Struggle Statement, 55

Emotions, discussion, 75–76

Empathy, display, 161, 163–164, 229

Employees
  building, leader (impact), 96
  challenges/problems, 100
  client-facing roles, 119
  commitment (improvement), wellness (increase), 6–7
  conversations, 157–158
  differences, attention, 116
  email, checking, 136
  empowerment, Rogerian approach, 158–160
  engagement, leader authenticity (impact), 27
  environment, creation, 164
  experience survey, 206
  feeling, perspective, 4–5
  Generator relationships, 8–9
  health/wellness, metrics tracking, 207

meeting, 161–162

mental health stigma, impact, 179–181

mentality, shift, 158

perspectives, valuation, 158

post-COVID-19 challenges, 23–24

preference, support, 120–121

productivity, increase, 27

reality, awareness, 24

retention, 123–124

satisfaction/engagement/ commitment, increase, 7

satisfaction/productivity, relationship, 5

success (support), flexible leadership (impact), 108–110

well employees, leader benefits, 8–10

Employee wellness

impact, 3–7

organizational support, 11–12

societal implications, 12–15

Engagement (increase), employee wellness (impact), 6

Extinguishers

control, 211–213

examples, sharing, 8

judgments, 167

knowledge, assumption, 204–205

leader examples, 27

role, 213–215

F

Feedback, providing, 48, 159, 184

Fire Your Work Self worksheet, 38

G

Generator Action Plan worksheet, 238–241

Generators

actions, 83

becoming, 25, 57, 68, 175, 197

behaviors

enactment, 147, 212

perspective, 60

recognition/acknowledgement, 212–213

support, gaining, 210

being, roadblocks, 172

details, sharing, 227

employee relationships, 8–9

example, 63–64

setting, 138

flexibility, 117–122, 200–201

goals, achievement, 10

language, importance, 187–189

mental health struggle statements, 183–187

person-centered approach, 168–169

positivity spread, 71–72

practicing, 63–65

prioritization ability, 206

recognitions, 171–172

role, 213–215

role models, 27

skill development, 154–155

struggles, 51, 181

team creativity/innovation, increase, 9–10

trust/relationship, building, 89

words, avoidance, 188

Goals

details, 235–236

measurement, 234

setting, 232–234

time-bound characteristic, 234

Go-to people, impact, 93

Gratitude
    characterization, 68
    contagiousness, 72–73
    daily gratitude practice, starting, 73
    power, recognition, 60
    practice, physical reminder (usage), 73
    spiral, 723
Gripe sessions, sharing (distinction), 47–48
Guilt, presence, 49

H
Habits, improvement, 76–77
Health, leader support, 2
Honesty, provocation, 229
Humanity
    culture, creation, 124–125
    driving, leader actions (impact), 125

I
Ideal worker persona, embodiment, 24
Ideas, brainstorming, 148
Inclusive language, usage, 182
Individuating information, impact, 87
Initiative, taking, 20–21
Integrating
    preference, capitalization, 114
    segmenting, contrast, 113
Integrators
    boundaries (setting), boundary bouncer (impact), 140–143
    interruptions, challenge, 115
    value, 114–117

    work-life boundaries, strictness (absence), 113–114
    work-life difference, 111–117
Intentional inquiry, 94–98

J
Judgment
    fear, 28
        absence, 170–171
    suspension, 161, 162–163, 229

K
Keep Track of Responses worksheet, 36

L
Language, importance (Generator knowledge), 187–189
Leaders
    actions, impact, 65–68
    authenticity
        employee need, 28–32
        impact, 27
    becoming, 197–198
    flexibility, 123–127
    impact, maximization, 67
    joy, focus, 66
    lives, focus, 65
    norms, evolution, 24
    planning/negotiation, 205–206
    professional norms, impact, 23–25
    pushback, 202
    reflection, 110
    relationships, building, 81
    stories, sharing (impact), 26
    struggle statement sharing, 50
    trust, 26–27

truthfulness, 186
vulnerability
  employee search, 25
  importance, 48
work self, presentation, 28
Leadership
  capabilities, 190
  feelings, fostering, 135
  team, expectations, 203
Learning disability, 170
Lives
  intentional inquiry, 94–98
  responsibilities, impact, 113
  segmentation/integration
    preferences, 116–117
  support, work (impact), 105,
    228–229
Loneliness, struggles, 23–24
Long-lasting friendships, 89–90

M

Mastery (recovery process),
  219–220
Maternity leave, usage, 118
Meaningful tokens, sharing, 91
Meeting objectives, 204
Mental health
  challenges, 230
  defining, 176
  disorder, 176
  employee education, 189–190
  issues, 214–215
  perspectives, 21
  problems, commonness, 177–181
  solution, leveraging, 178–179
  struggles, 23–24
    statements, Generator usage,
      183–187
    vulnerabilities, conveying, 184

support, Generators (impact),
  181–191
Mental health stigma
  elimination, 175, 182
  experience, 180
  impact, 179–181
  reality, 177–179
Mental wellness, critique, 64
Metrics, tracking, 202, 206–209
Mindset shift, 154, 159
Miscommunication (reduction),
  SWIFT process (impact), 87
Misconceptions (reduction), SWIFT
  process (impact), 86–87
Misunderstandings (reduction),
  SWIFT process (impact),
  87–88

N

Narratives, damage (reversal), 159
Negative behaviors, origin, 214–215
Negative emotions, expression, 76
Neurodivergent employees, health/
  well-being/performance,
  169–170
Note-taking, acceptability, 99

O

Objective data, usage, 208
One-on-one conversation, impact,
  88–89, 205, 214
One-on-one meetings, 47, 50, 69,
  90, 97
Open conversations, impact,
  217–218
Opportunity, identification
  (difficulty), 233
Outcomes, measurement, 208
Overwork, cultures, 230

combating, 198–211
overcoming, 199
toxicity, 201–202
Overwork, focus, 199–200

P

Paid time off (PTO) model, 201
Peer team goals, 203
Perfectionists, unapproachability,
    20–23
Performance, problem, 62
Personal/difficult insights,
    sharing, 22
Personal struggles, handling, 21
Personal time, interruption, 146
Person-centered approach, 168–169
Person-centered planning
    importance, reason, 165–171
    learning, 155–156
    power, 153, 170–171
    practice, 167
        Generator, impact, 154–155
    Rogerian approach, 156–165
    steps, 161–165
Physical illness, incurrence, 178
Positive culture
    falseness, 75
    maintenance, 72
Positive emotions
    contagiousness, 69–70
    impact, 70–71
Positivity
    origin, 68
    power, recognition, 60, 69
Post-one-on-one reflection, 100
Power of Person-Centered Planning
    worksheet, 173–174
Prioritization, skill, 202–203
Probing questions, usage, 94–98

Problem solving strategies, creation,
    171
Productivity, promotion, 165–166
Prosocial conformity, 74

Q

Questions, usage (caution), 95

R

Reciprocity culture, creation, 73
Recovery
    activities (engagement neglect),
        Integrators (impact), 141
    strategies/skills, 218–221
Relationship-building sprints, time
    allotment, 88–90
Relationships
    building, 93
        Generator, impact, 98
    trust, growth, 89–90
    understanding, 100
Relaxation, recovery process,
    218–219
Rogerian approach, 156–165
    creation, 160
    difficulty, 157–158
Rogers, Carl, 156
Role modeling, impact, 74–76

S

Segmenters
    boundaries (setting),
        boundary bouncer
        (impact), 140–143
    employees, support, 114
    roles, boundaries, 115
    value, 114–117
Self-defense mode, 37–38

Self-improvement, reflection (time allotment), 98–100
Self-protection, brainstorming, 148
Self-reflection, 38–39
Self-sustaining culture, building, 67
Self-worth, regard/preservation, 157–158
Sentiments, exclusion, 184
Set the Right Tone worksheet, 78–79
Setting aside time, Welcoming, Intentionally inquiring, Following up, Taking time (SWIFT) process, 85f, 90, 154–155, 228
  impact, 86–87
  importance, reason, 84–88
  usage, 84–100
Sharing, impact, 49–50
Skillset, leveling up, 155
Social isolation, struggles, 23–24
Specific, Measurable, Achievable, Relevant, and Time-bound (SMART), 233–234
Spreadsheet, building, 204
Stigma
  active reduction, Generators (impact), 182
  occurrence, 176–177
Stress, increase (survey results), 64–65
Struggles, sharing
  distinction, 47–48
  power, 46
Struggle statements, 227
  construction, 40–41
  defining, 39–45
  embracing, 37
  example, 41–44

Generator sharing, 49
  importance, 44–45
  integration, 52
  sharing, 50, 51–53, 183–184
  usage, reasons, 45–48
Subcultures, creation, 143–145
Success pathways, Generator recognition, 110
Superheros, necessity (absence), 17, 226–227
Survey, development, 207
SWIFT Become a Confidant worksheet, 103–104
Sympathy, impact, 163–164

T
Team cultures
  creation, 75
  Generator creation, 59–60
  instilling, 66
  positive emotions, 70
Teammate, support, 68
Teams
  creativity/innovation, increase, 9–10
  energy, shift, 22
  environment, creation, 69
  goals, achievement, 10
  honesty, power (recognition), 185
  members
    Generator flexibility/support, 216
  members, struggles, 19–20
  personal trauma, secrecy, 21
  progress, challenges, 53
  protection, 145
  vulnerability, building, 183–184
  workload, reprioritization, 205–206

Time
  allotment, 88–90
  investment, 155–156
Tone, setting, 59, 212, 227–228
  Generators, impact, 74
Trust
  building/growth, 26, 89–90
  focus, shift, 158
Trusting relationships, building, 124–125
Trustworthiness, judgments, 88

V
"Value the whole person," 112
Vital few, focus, 202–206
Vulnerability
  benefits, 186–187
  display, 39, 182, 184
  impact, 50
Vulnerable leader, employee need, 45

W
Weaknesses, sharing, 46
Welcoming (SWIFT process), 90–93
Well employees, impact, 8–10
Wellness
  focus, company benefit, 3
  impact, 2, 11–12
  importance, perspectives, 2–3
  increase, 6–7
  leader support, 2
  prioritization, 142–143
  promotion, 165–166

What-ifs, consideration, 119–122
Withdrawal behaviors, 7
Worker norms, pervasiveness, 61–62
Work-family conflict
  meaning, 139
  struggles, 23–24
Working styles, accommodation (Generator action), 117
Work-life balance, 233
  culture, creation, 228
  Generator valuation, 229
  modeling, 60–68
  support, company policies (absence), 121–122
Work-life boundaries, setting (leader support), 135
Work-life difference, 111–117
Workload, prioritization, 205–206
Workplace
  dynamics, 158–159
  flexibility, 200
  inclusivity, 83
Workplace wellness
  importance, 1, 226
  outcome, 1–2
  passion, 3
Workr Beeing, 12–13
Work-related stress, outside impact, 13
Work-related struggles, 40
Work-related weaknesses, sharing, 38